BUY-TO-LET

HOW TO GET STARTED

ROB SMALLBONE

POWERHOUSE
PUBLICATIONS

COPYRIGHT

Powerhouse Publications
Unit 124. 94 London Road
Headington, Oxford
OX3 9FN

www.powerhousepublishing.com

With thanks to Mouseprice.com and Rightmove.com.
All images are used with the permission of the owners.
Thank you to the following estate agents for allowing their name, number and logo to be published: Gordon Brown, Property & Invest, Marlborough and Living Local.

TESTIMONIALS

"Having been in this property business for a little while now, I have always made time to read books written by investors for hints and tips that I have yet to consider in my own journey.

Having read Rob's book, I can honestly say I have not come across a more comprehensive and thorough book. If you are already in the business, this book will no doubt give you more ideas, not just on property but in life. Whilst it is geared to people who are new to property and, specifically buy-to-let properties, there will be hints and tips that you will take away from this to use in all aspects of property investment.

If you are new to property or are thinking that you really should be getting involved in property, then this book will honestly be your bible!

The content covered in this book is exactly what you would find from a course costing thousands and all the notes you would make have been made for you. In essence, you will save money with this book and you will no doubt make money. Rob will walk you step by step through the entire process, so you know exactly what you should be doing from the start to completion. Get it, study it and learn from it, do the actions (all explained meticulously) and you will achieve exactly what you need to in order to reach your goals in the future."

– Matthew Colburn, Seeded Property Solutions

"Rob has put his extensive knowledge into a very accessible style of writing; very simple and straightforward. An amazing amount of content has been provided for free that many others would charge you for. New to property investing, this is a great place to start. I would recommend it to anyone!"

– Aaron Devoy, Risk and Compliance Manager at Avantis Wealth

DEDICATION

I would like to dedicate this book to you, the reader, for believing in me and the content that you are about to read. It is an honour, pleasure and privilege to be able to write this for you so that you are able to continue (or start) building your own property portfolio. Your support (and continued support) really is appreciated.

There are four special mentions though:

Thank you to Aaron Devoy (co-founder of Devoy & Smallbone Properties) for putting up with my petulance throughout the writing of this book. I promise that our co-authored travelling book will be much easier to write!

Thank you to Matt McSherry (co-founder of The Property Nomads) for continually believing in me and driving me towards to the finishing line, metaphorically speaking.

Thank you to Rachael Taylor (director at The Property Nomads). Your belief in me is fantastic and thank you for joining in on The Property Nomads Journey at such a fascinating time!

To Mum, your second favourite child (I know my place in life :D) has written a book! I know that you are proud of both your children and we are, and will always be, driven by your unfettered and never-ending love. Thank you.

Table of Contents

Foreword

It is an honour and a privilege to be able to write this book for you. At the time of writing, I have accumulated over 20 properties in just over three years, 16 of which are buy-to-lets. I therefore feel as though enough experience has been gained to warrant writing a book in order to show you what you too can achieve in property.

Usually, you will see numerous success stories of people that have hit the jackpot within 12 months of investing in property. For those people who do that, many congratulations. In reality, property should be considered to be a long-term wealth creation strategy and an asset accumulation vehicle that, like many other businesses, has its pros and cons.

This book is designed to give you a step-by-step guide to buying your first buy-to-let property in the UK. It is designed to provide as much advice as possible without giving you the false impression that property is 'plain sailing', 'easy' and 'straightforward'. There are many instances where people seemingly get sold a dream that property is a walk in the park.

Property is good fun. It can be very easy, yet you should not be under any illusion that it is straightforward 100% of the time. There will be good times and there will be bad times. As with anything in life, it is down to your mentality in order to take the good with the bad, the rough with the smooth, and the highs with the lows.

To reiterate, property is not a get-rich-quick scheme. Property takes time and whilst there are instances where people can achieve a lot of success in a short space of time, it is important to point out that these instances are unusual.

There are property strategies that can enhance your cashflow and enable you to achieve your financial freedom and life goals quicker. Buy-to-let is not one of those strategies. Buy-to-lets will provide you with a bedrock of knowledge, and are often the best strategy to start with.

Therefore, please do not read this book and automatically think that you will get rich quick just through buy-to-lets. Over time, after reading this book, I am positive that you will grow a successful portfolio and it will continue to thrive.

This dose of reality just had to be put in because so many people get emotionally hyped after attending a course, reading a book or listening to a podcast and, as a result, get false expectations of the property industry.

All good things come to those to wait and those are prepared to be consistently persistent in order to achieve their goals.

A lot of times in this book I'll mention that 'there is no right or wrong way'. By this, I mean that the decision to do something is ultimately yours. In other words, if you decide to manage the refurb of a property, then that is up to you. If you decide to do the refurb yourself to gain experience, then that is up to you as well.

As a budding investor, it is a belief of mine that as long as you do everything under the 'ethical umbrella' – i.e. you do not cut corners or be a bad landlord/landlady, then there is no right or wrong way of growing your property portfolio.

Throughout this book, there will be opinions on tax, property investment methods and ways in which to set up your property business. It is very important to state that I am not personally regulated by the FCA, so the opinions that you will read are just opinions and they are not constituted to be financial advice or construed to be advice which you should act upon.

Your financial and tax positions will be different from mine and therefore it is highly recommended that you seek the necessary professional advice in order to get everything set up in a way that is most suitable and efficient for you.

Who Am I?

I am co-founder of Devoy & Smallbone Properties and The Property Nomads. I co-host The Property Nomads Podcast with Matt McSherry. The podcast provides a blend of property, travel and business-related information, tips and tricks and interviews with a variety of business and property people. The podcast is currently in over 55 countries and, at the time of writing, has over 7,500 downloads and over 500 subscribers. The podcast will continue to grow and I thank you in advance for you support!

You can subscribe to The Property Nomads Podcast for FREE on:

iTunes – https://apple.co/2UdfXXY

Stitcher – https://bit.ly/2uC2RVr

Spotify – https://spoti.fi/2Wvxk3I

The Property Nomads Podcast is on most podcast platforms so come and check us out, subscribe and share with your friends and family.

I am also on the committee for The Humber Landlords' Association. The HLA is a private landlord group based in Kingston upon Hull and covers the Hull, Grimsby and Scunthorpe areas. Although area specific, the HLA is a recognisable property body, much like the National Landlords' Association (NLA) and the Residential Landlords' Association (RLA).

As mentioned already, my business partners and I have accumulated 20 properties in just over three years – 16 of which are buy-to-lets – with an asset value just over £1million. Over £500,000 of joint venture finance has been successfully raised too. It is only when you truly take time to look back at something that you realise how much has been achieved.

I've had two stints at travelling: February to April 2011, and then June 2014 to March 2015. In between the travelling, I was working as a security guard at The Oracle shopping centre in Reading. The job was thoroughly enjoyable and we had a good community of people there, yet I knew that I was purposely saving to visit Brazil for the 2014 FIFA World Cup.

It is fair to say that the turning point was in July 2011 when my stepdad was diagnosed with a rare form of brain cancer. He died in September 2011. This left a lot of people dumbfounded and it was only after the dust had settled on what had just happened that I realised that my mum had never completed her bucket list with him because they thought that they would live for a lot longer.

This was incredibly eye-opening and I vowed from that point on never to miss out on an opportunity and never to use 'money' as an excuse for doing so.

In 2011, I had not yet met property and property had not yet met me, hence the continuation of working to go travelling.

The travelling was incredibly exciting and invigorating. Hand on heart, I can truly say that travelling changed me as a person. That's a whole other book in itself though, so watch this space!

Who This Book Is For

Have you already invested in property? Are you fed up with your current job and want to make a change in your life? Are you looking to get into another business in order to transform your life? Do you want to make yourself money rather than make other people money?

If you do, then you are definitely in the right place.

This book has been written for those who are thinking of, or interested in, getting into property yet do not know where to start.

This book has been written for those who are struggling with the confidence to buy their first investment property, those who have attended any property training seminars or courses yet have not purchased their first property, and for those who are 'flustered' by information overload and need a guiding hand and some focus in order to move forward and succeed.

Maybe you are already successfully investing in property and want a bit more of an insight into buy-to-let investing or you are looking at ways to improve your portfolio. If that is the case, then you are definitely reading the right book too!

This book will not be for everyone. Whilst there is a plethora of knowledge to be shared and gained from reading this book, if you are already a very successful buy-to-let investor then you may struggle to pick up new information or something you don't know already.

The Aim of This Book

The aim is to provide you with a step-by-step process so that you are able to buy your first buy-to-let property in the UK. This will be done by being as in-depth as possible.

- You will go on a journey.
- You will challenge your mind.
- You will find out and work out why you want to invest in property.
- You will work out what your vision is.

- You will find out what your values and dreams are.
- You will also discover where in the UK to purchase buy-to-let properties.

From figuring out where in the UK to purchase buy-to-let property, you will then learn:

- How to view properties.
- How to work out the numbers on the property, such as the yields.
- How to work out cashflow from each property.
- How to buy, renovate, let and refinance.

You will learn all of this and you should then have a really thorough guide to be able to take that step of investing.

After reading this book, you should be better equipped mentally in order to either start your property journey or to continue investing successfully.

Having invested over £20,000 to kickstart my property education and training, having a step-by-step guide book at the start would have been ideal, hence the desire to write this for you.

This book will start with an in-depth section on mindset and goal-setting before going through the nooks and crannies of buy-to-let property investing.

Structure Of The Book

First of all, the book will explore mindset and the importance of having a good mentality when it comes to property investing. Goal setting is explored in an in-depth manner too and exercises are provided so that you can set your goals and understand why it is you have decided to invest in property.

From there, we go on a journey. We will explore:

- The most suitable methods for buy-to-let investing.
- Which areas to avoid.
- How to work out your returns.
- The 20-step process of how to buy a property.
- What to look for when buying property.
- How to successfully tenant the property.

There will be a summary of each section covered and there are plenty of hints, tips and tricks throughout the book too!

The book will be as realistic as possible. There are too many people out there that paint this picture of property always being full of pots of gold, rainbows and leprechauns. I'm here to tell you that while that is certainly possible and achievable, reality suggests that property is a lot nittier and grittier than that. Therefore, a dose of reality will occur in this book in order to paint a fairer picture for you.

Differences in Legislation and Buying Processes

There are a couple of important things to note:

1. The buying process in Scotland is slightly different to that in England. This is not covered in this book purely because I have never bought in Scotland.
2. Various laws and legislations can be different in England, Wales, Scotland and Northern Ireland. Where possible, I have tried to distinguish between them all.
3. The main focus in the book is England, so apologies if anything regarding Wales, Scotland or Northern Ireland is missed out. This is not intentional.

Mindset – Why Mindset Is Important

You may or may not have done some property training before, listened to a property podcast, sat through a property webinar or indeed have read another property-related book. If you have had the pleasure of doing any of these activities, then no doubt they will have touched on mindset.

Mindset is fundamental to anything that you do in life. The first part of this book will focus on mindset and it is important that you do all the activities!

Time has to be taken to win the battle that goes on in your head. Once you win that battle, then you will be setting yourself up nicely for many successes.

Property is not always as straightforward as people make it out to be. There will be days where things go right and there will definitely be days where things go wrong.

Having a strong mindset and a wealth mindset will help you to oversee the negatives that will happen in the property world.

For myself, travelling helped me. I was fortunate enough to go to the FIFA World Cup in Brazil in 2014 (through working and saving hard, not through the accumulation of assets) and then I travelled to South and Central America for the ensuing 10 months. I can safely say that travelling changed my mindset and was the best decision that I have ever made.

Before I went to Brazil, I was closed-minded, angry, not spontaneous, materialistic, very emotional and felt like the world was against me. Having time with my mind, having seen people who didn't have a lot of possessions, yet with bigger smiles on their faces (and seemingly a better quality of life as a result) really shook me to the core.

Experiencing other cultures, languages and belief systems is pretty much priceless in terms of what that can do for your mind.

From those 10 months traversing South and Central America, I came back more energised, more open-minded, less materialistic and way more appreciative of what I had in my life at the time. The time to travel is my underlying 'why' when it comes to property investing, because travel opened my eyes to bigger ways of thinking, a new way of life and a new understanding of how the world works. In turn, that led me to property.

Although you don't have to go travelling in order to find yourself, all of us will have an epiphany moment at some point in our lives. That moment will bring about a seismic shift in mindset.

Mindset – Why You Must Have A Why

Having a 'why' will be integral to your success in property. It is crucial that you take time to sit down and think about this section as it will change your life and your way of thinking.

This may seem like an exercise that you do not want to do – yet it is very, very effective and very rewarding.

Think about some pain points in your life at the moment. Are you working 40–50 hours per week in a job that you don't like? Are you working to make other people richer and not yourself?

Are you finding that you do not spend as much time with your spouse or children as you should do? Would you like more time to travel? Do you have a bucket list that you are nowhere near to achieving?

Do you want to leave a legacy for your family?

Do you just want more money? I.e. your financial freedom

These are some of the most common pain points with people who are looking to invest in property.

Sit down somewhere with no distractions and focus on why you are going to invest in property.

Take time to come up with the top 5 reasons:

1. ....

....

....

2. ....

....

....

3. ....

....

....

4. ....

....

....

5. ....

....

....

Now you have your top 5 reasons, you need to work out your main reason; your burning desire.

Most people say that they are seeking 'financial freedom'.

From experience, this is normally just a gateway to a much bigger reason. For example:

- To travel the world.
- To spend more time with your family.

- To have the time to do things.
- To create a legacy for your family.
- To have a sense of freedom.
- To have choices.

Your reason may be one of the above. Your reason may be completely different. Your reason should be personal and should give you a burning desire. Now is the time to be honest with yourself – dig deep down and take time to really think about your why.

....

....

....

....

....

....

....

....

....

....

....

For me, it is all about having the time freedom and flexibility to do what I want when I want. This works hand in hand with wanting to visit every country in the world by the time I am 50. At this current point in time, I'm 45 countries in (out of circa 200) and showing no signs of slowing down.

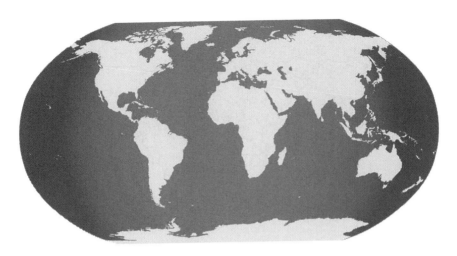

Your why will mean the world to you and it will not matter what anyone else thinks about it. Your why is your burning desire, your why will get you out of bed in the morning, your why will help you to see you through those tough times and your why will help to keep you focused when all around you seems like it is falling apart.

You don't have to share your why with anyone else if you do not want to.

Make sure that your why is powerful as it will need to get you through the tough times. I have had times where properties have been vandalised by tenants and by people off the street. These times were testing mentally, but knowing why I got into property (financial and time freedom, along with travel) helped me through.

It would have been very easy to have thrown my toys out of the pram on those occasions, to have chucked in the towel and to have quit but I did not. Sh*t happens in property. It is part of the fun and is part of the ups and downs that you will experience along the way.

Mindset – What Is Your Financial Freedom Figure?

NB. All these figures are per month

Once you have your why, then it is good to know what your ideal financial freedom figure is.

Once you have your financial freedom figure, then it becomes easier to set strategically sensible goals. In other words, how many properties you need in order to reach that figure.

Spreadsheets might not be your favourite thing in the world (they are definitely not mine) yet to have control over your finances and knowledge of what you spend money on, month in and month out, they will put you in good stead.

Ideally, you will want to create a simple sheet in Excel that looks something like this:

Income	Amount	Expense	Amount
Total	£ -	Total	£ -

The idea is to then list all the things that bring you income in per month and all of the expenses that you have per month. This is designed to be your PERSONAL expenses. This is because if you are not in control of your personal expenses, then you will never be in control of your business expenses.

Income	Amount	Expense	Amount
Net Wages	£ 2,000.00	Accommodation/Mortgage	£ 600.00
		Council Tax	£ 130.00
		Water	£ 40.00
		Gas + Electric	£ 100.00
		Internet	£ 50.00
		House Insurance	£ 20.00

Income	Amount	Expense	Amount
		TV Licence	£ 15.00
		Phone	£ 60.00
		Food	£ 200.00
		Gym	£ 50.00
		Entertainment	£ 300.00
		Clothing	£ 100.00
		Car/Fuel	£ 300.00
Total	£ 2,000.00	Total	£ 1,965.00

The above is just an example. You may spend less on food per month and more on the gym, the important thing is that you do this exercise so that you know how much money is going in and out per month.

In property, sacrifices have to be made. Would you rather eat out less per month for a couple of years until you've bought a couple of properties that can pay for those very meals?

Everyone is different and there is no right or wrong. However, it is very common to see that successful property investors have made sacrifices at some stage.

People sometimes complain that they have too much month left at the end of the money, yet those exact people may be wasting £1,000 a month on their lavish lifestyles – too many holidays, too much fine dining, etc. Some little tweaks here and there and you'll be able to save for a deposit for a buy-to-let! (You can also raise the finance from investors, but more on that later).

After you have done that exercise, then you will have a better understanding of your financial freedom figure. Using the previous table, let's say that entertainment, food and clothing can be decreased. In other words, you have enough to pay for the essentials but not for luxuries such as those extra takeaways or those extra beers with your mates.

Income	Amount	Expense	Amount
Net Wages	£ 2,000.00	Accommodation/Mortgage	£ 600.00
		Council Tax	£ 130.00
		Water	£ 40.00
		Gas + Electric	£ 100.00
		Internet	£ 50.00
		House Insurance	£ 20.00
		TV Licence	£ 15.00
		Phone	£ 60.00
		Food	£ 100.00
		Gym	£ 50.00
		Entertainment	£ 100.00
		Clothing	£ 50.00
		Car/Fuel	£ 300.00
Total	£ 2,000.00	Total	£ 1,615.00

You can see that the expenses have dropped from £1,965 to £1,615 per month. If you are able to trim back your expenses then you will have your 'basic financial freedom figure'. This is a great start. Your basic financial freedom figure is the basic amount that you need to live on per month. You could easily reduce your entertainment etc. down to £0 but for the purposes of this book, and reality, you will want to keep sane by having some fun each month!

Any good buy-to-let property in the north should cashflow at least £200 per month. In the south, this may be different as you may buy for capital growth rather than cashflow (more on this later), but we will assume that you want to quit your job and build your own portfolio for the cashflow.

Some simple maths (1,615/200 = 8.075) shows that you will need 8.075 buy-to-let properties in order to achieve your basic financial freedom. In reality, this will be nine properties as acquiring 0.075 of a property could be quite a challenge!

Once you have done this, then you need to know what your ultimate financial freedom figure is. Through the exercises that you have already done, you may want £3,000 per month so that you can live in a nice house, have a couple of extra holidays a year and not have to work any more.

Let's assume a figure of £3,000 per month (as this is quite a common figure amongst investors) then (£3,000/£200 = 15) will mean that you need to acquire 15 cash-flowing buy-to-lets.

Your aspirations may look something like this:

Income	Amount	Expense	Amount
Property Portfolio	£3,000.00	Accommodation/Mortgage	£ 800.00
		Council Tax	£ 130.00
		Water	£ 40.00
		Gas + Electric	£ 100.00
		Internet	£ 50.00
		House Insurance	£ 20.00
		TV Licence	£ 15.00
		Phone	£ 60.00
		Food	£ 300.00

Income	Amount	Expense	Amount
		Gym	£ 50.00
		Entertainment	£ 500.00
		Clothing	£ 350.00
		Car/Fuel	£ 500.00
		Professional Clubs	£ 85.00
Total	£3,000.00	Total	£ 3,000.00

You may want to earn £10,000 a month (50 cash-flowing buy-to-lets as £10,000/£200 = 50) so that you can permanently travel and be more opulent and extravagant with your life choices. There is no right or wrong.

At £10,000, your aspirations may look something like this:

Income	Amount	Expense	Amount
Property Portfolio	£ 10,000.00	Accommodation/ Mortgage	£ 1,500.00
		Council Tax	£ 250.00
		Water	£ 50.00
		Gas + Electric	£ 250.00
		Internet	£ 100.00
		House Insurance	£ 100.00
		TV Licence	£ 20.00
		Phone	£ 100.00
		Food	£ 300.00

Income	Amount	Expense	Amount
		Gym	£ 50.00
		Entertainment	£ 830.00
		Clothing	£ 450.00
		Car/Fuel	£ 500.00
		Professional Clubs	£ 500.00
		Holidays	£ 1,500.00
		School Fees	£ 1,500.00
		Other Investment	£ 2,000.00
Total	£ 10,000.00	Total	£ 10,000.00

Again, there is no right or wrong and your life is your life. The important part is that you go through these exercises so that you know your 'why', you know what will drive you to succeed, you know your basic financial freedom figure and your long-term financial freedom figure so that you have the lifestyle you want and you know you deserve.

Mindset – The Importance Of Setting Goals And How To Set Effective Goals Across All Walks Of Life

Why you should set goals

Did you know that approximately 3% of the world's wealth is owned by 97% of the population and that 3% of the world's population owns 97% of the world's wealth?

Just think about that for a minute.

Some of us do not have choices in life as we may live in countries that do not allow our freedom or there may be other circumstances that mean that we are not mentally capable for whatever reason.

However, for the rest of us that do have that ability, that statistic is very compelling and does pose one big question: how can some people become wealthy and others become poor?

For example, look at very successful individuals such as Elon Musk, Sir Richard Branson, Tony Robbins and Jeff Bezos. All of those individuals have two things in common:

1. They all have 24 hours in a day.
2. They have set themselves massive goals

What you do in your 24 hours a day is up to you. There are a lot of people that will set up successful businesses despite working 50–60 hours a week, and there are some people who work 35 hours or less a week and struggle to set up successful businesses because they do not use their time efficiently.

If you do not have goals, then you will not know what you are aiming for. You do not want to get stuck in a state of analysis paralysis and nor do you want to just motor on through life without any sense of dedication and direction.

The fact that you are reading this book shows that you are either on the goal-setting and success path already or that you do not want to let yourself motor along any more and that you want a change!

Very successful entrepreneurs and individuals such as Sir Richard Branson and Tony Robbins have set themselves huge goals and have known what they are aiming for at all times. This has given them a sense of purpose, clarity and vision and they have been able to create many businesses and vast wealth as a result.

You can do this too if you know what you want and why you want it!

The Seven Areas Of Life That You Need To Set Goals In

There are seven areas in life in which you should set goals. All of them go hand in hand: it is essential that you take the time to think about your life as it is now and what you want it to be like moving forward. Also, think about creating a legacy and a very long-term plan (such as a 25-year plan).

1. Business/Work
2. Personal Wealth
3. Energy
4. Mental
5. Physical
6. Spiritual
7. Emotional/Social

Some of these areas may not seem as important as others. If you think like this, then you will have an imbalance in your life and this is not a good thing. In order to become successful, you will need plans and goals in your life and you will need to treat each of these seven areas as seriously as the others.

In order to help you, I've created a template that you can utilise in Excel:

Life Plan	1 year	2 years	5 years	10 years	25 years
Business/Work					
Personal Wealth					
Energy					
Mental					
Physical					
Spiritual					
Emotional/Social					

From your Life Plan, then create a Monthly Success List:

Monthly Success List	(Insert Month Here)	Goals
Business/Work		
Personal Wealth		
Energy		
Mental		
Physical		
Spiritual		
Emotional/Social		

From the Monthly Success List, create a Weekly Success List:

Weekly Success List	(Insert Week Here)	Goals
Business/Work		
Personal Wealth		
Energy		
Mental		
Physical		
Spiritual		
Emotional/Social		

From the Weekly Success List, create a Daily Success List:

Daily Success List	(Insert Day Here)	Goals
Business/Work		
Personal Wealth		

Daily Success List	(Insert Day Here)	Goals
Energy		
Mental		
Physical		
Spiritual		
Emotional/Social		

Once you have created these templates and adapted them to suit yourself, then take the time to think about your life, your future and what you want. All seven areas take time, and some useful questions to consider have been listed beneath each section. These are questions and thoughts that have helped me to plan my life and goals.

1. Business/Work

Business/work is very important. Business/work takes up a large chunk of our lives in one way or another.

There are important questions that you will need to ask yourself when setting your goals:

- What is it you want to achieve?
- What will your legacy be?

- How many properties do you want?
- What cash-flow do you want?
- Do you want multiple streams of property income?
- Where do you see your business in five years' time?
- Do you want any employees?
- Do you want to be the CEO of the company that you work for?
- Do you want your current boss's job?
- What will people remember you or your business for?

Having an understanding of what you are looking to achieve in the long-term will help you to create suitable goals for the short and medium term.

For example, in property, if you want to have 50 buy-to-let properties after 10 years, then a realistic target would be to add five per year. If you are completely new to property then you might decide to purchase two in the first year, three in the second year, six in the third year and so forth until you get to your target.

2. Personal Wealth

Personal Wealth is not necessarily about the amount of money that you have in your pocket but the lifestyle that you are leading or that you want to lead and have.

Some people are driven by financial freedom and making as much money as possible. For others, the financial freedom enables them to have time freedom which in turn enables them to pursue other activities such as setting up charities, being able to work on bigger projects for fun, having more time with the family or travelling the world.

Knowing why you are doing what you are doing and how you want your life to be will be a big help in the personal wealth section. Think about the following questions:

- How much money would you like per month?
- What will financial freedom bring to you?
- Are you after time freedom?
- Do you want to travel the world?
- Would you like more time with your family?
- What is very important to you in your life?
- What do you aspire to be and to have?

Everyone is different and everyone will have their different reasons. Just saying "financial freedom" or "time freedom" isn't good enough as there will always be an underlying reason as to why you want and need those things.

3. Energy

Energy is about being inspired and doing things that you like to do. For some people this may mean going on holiday, and for others it may mean activities such as going out to a lovely restaurant, drawing, reading, playing chess or resting.

When thinking of your energy goals ask yourself the following questions:

- What gives you that buzz?
- What would you like to reward yourself with?
- When was the last time you did something fun?
- What do you like to do that gives you a big buzz?
- What would be an ultimate reward for you?
- Are you missing excitement in your life?
- Do you feel stressed?

If you are feeling stressed or overwhelmed, then chances are that you have not had enough fun. Anything that brings you excitement or helps you to be able to relax needs to be in the energy section.

4. Mental

This is about mindset, how you think and your mental ability to believe that you can achieve your dreams and desires. It is about feeding your brain with podcasts, Audible books, reading and brain-training materials.

Ask yourself these key questions when considering mental goals.

- How many books can you read in a year?
- How many podcasts can you listen to in a year?
- How many audio books can you listen to in a year?
- Have you exercised your brain recently?
- What skills would you like to learn?
- How many different personal growth events can you attend in a year?

Mental health is crucial. If you are able to test your brain on a regular basis by playing chess, doing a difficult puzzle, reading, learning or any cognitive activities, then this will help you in the long run because you will be able to solve challenges in life and business too.

Try listening to podcasts or audiobooks (check out Audible) and attend more events. Really test your brain and mental health by getting your brain thinking and exploring.

5. Physical

Physical health is very important. You have probably heard the phrase that good health equals good wealth.

Think about your body, your shape, how you feel, what you look like and what you want to look like. Think about the food you eat, your diet and your physical strength. How can you improve these areas?

Do you have a lifelong dream to climb a mountain?

Do you want to run a marathon?

If you have good health and you exercise regularly, then you will know that the endorphins are released into your system and they lead to more positive vibes, which can lead to more productivity.

Having an active brain that is thinking will enable you to be creative and it will also enable you to find solutions for difficult challenges that you might be facing in your life and in your business.

The motivational speaker and author, Jim Rohn, said, *"It is easy to do and it is easy not to do."*

Do not neglect the physical side at all.

If you do not enjoy much physical exercise, then look to make the small changes in your life such as using the stairs instead of the lift or the escalator, or parking at the end of the supermarket car park so you have to walk further to get to the supermarket.

All these little changes build up over time and snowball into a big effect and will have a big effect on your life. Doing the little things over the course of time will create a butterfly effect. In the future, you will look back on all the small changes that you have made and thank yourself for making them.

6. Spiritual

This is an area which people will often neglect as they believe that having a spiritual aspect to them will not help at all. It is always good to have a bit of a spiritual outlook as this will help shape your mentality, shape how you see the world and shape your overall emotional balance.

Being at one with yourself and the way in which you are able to view life is very important and a key to being successful. If you are spiritually stable, then you will be able to be emotionally stable. Emotional stability leads to better decision making, which leads to success and growth.

Having good spiritual health level doesn't necessarily have to be about 10-day silent retreats in the middle of Cambodia. It can simply be about undertaking breathing exercises for five minutes, de-fogging your brain space for 10 minutes or being thankful in a journal.

A superb book to buy or listen to on Audible is 'As a Man Thinketh' by James Allen.

I have a morning gratitude journal and an evening daily summary journal. I find that taking some time out every morning before I start my day and being able to show gratitude (whether that be for knowing how to write, having somewhere to live, etc.) really helps me to set myself up properly for the day ahead. Reflecting in the evenings is very useful exercise too.

7. Emotional/Social

Emotional health is all about your relationships with others and what you can do to improve them. Relationships with others will include your spouse, your children, business partners, parents, friends and others.

- How do you feel about your current relationships?
- Could you be a better person in your relationships?
- How do you treat strangers that you meet?

- What first impression do you give?
- How are your relationships in general?
- Could your relationships be better?

Setting goals in the emotional section could be about improving your current relationships or working on creating a better first impression or attending new networking events.

How To Effectively Set Goals Using The SMART Methodology

In order to set your goals efficiently in those seven areas, I recommend that you follow the SMART methodology.

By using the SMART methodology, you will be able to successfully and incrementally implement your goals.

SMART stands for:

Specific

- What is it that you are after?
- What is the end goal?
- What do you want to achieve?

Meaningful

- Why is it important to you?

Action Orientated

- What steps will you take to achieve your goal?

Realistic

- How do you know that you can achieve this goal? (i.e if you are looking to run a marathon and do not currently run at all, then is it realistic to run a marathon in six weeks?)

Time Frame

- When do you want to achieve this goal?

Using the example of 50 buy-to-let properties, you may want to build a portfolio of 50 within a 10-year period by adding five per year. You will know why it is meaningful to you and that it is realistic by talking to other people. Your action points may be to view houses, offer on houses, raise finance and attend networking events. Your goal is specific (50 in 10 years) and has a time frame (10 years).

Setting goals using the SMART methodology will take time. It is not designed to be an exercise that will take 10 minutes. Enjoy setting your goals and taking the time to do it. Use the Life Planner, Monthly, Weekly and Daily success planners in order to help you.

Summary

Incredibly wealthy and successful people have set goals throughout their lives, so setting goals can change your life too. We all have 24 hours in a day. We all have the same time, yet what we do with that time will help us to determine our lives.

If you do not set goals, then you will not know what you are aiming for and you will just motor along through life without a sense of purpose or fulfilment.

Having a time frame is crucial to your success. Knowing your end game (eg. 50 buy-to-lets in 10 years) is very beneficial as you will be able to work backwards to such an extent where you will know what you have to do on a week-by-week basis in order to achieve what you want to achieve in the long term.

Take some time to think about what you really want to achieve in your life.

Rob's Recommended Top 7 Mindset Books That You Need To Read!

There are so many books out there. So much information. So many new things to learn. So many things to read.

This list is NOT a definitive list. It is simply the top seven mindset books that I believe you need to read (or listen to, if you prefer to do so, on Audible).

If you spoke to 100 different people and asked them to name their top seven mindset books, then it is very likely that you will get 100 different combinations.

Every book in this list is useful in its own right.

I've provided a brief summary on each of these seven books.

1. *The Chimp Paradox* by Prof. Steve Peters

Every one of us has a chimp inside us. This chimp rules our emotions while we humans just go along with what the chimp says and does. The chimp is in charge. Or is it?

Prof. Steve Peters breaks down the fact that we humans are in control of our brain, our thoughts and our reactions in different situations. We all have a human, a chimp and a computer aspect inside our brain. Most of the time, the chimp wins and that is not good for anyone involved.

Humans are rational – it is the chimp that is emotional, yet the chimp always seems to prevail.

Learn how to deal with this emotional chimp so that you too can make better and more effective decisions whilst disengaging from this 'red mist' that most of us get from time to time.

This book is a must-read and certainly helped me change the way I think and react in certain situations.

2. *Secrets of the Millionaire Mind* by T. Harv Eker

What makes the millionaire mind different from just a regular mind? T. Harv Eker will reveal the secrets in this book. It is phenomenal to know how your brain and mind works differently when you are thinking about big numbers, big dreams and big visions.

We are all capable of achieving such heights. It is just that our mindset is sometimes not in the right place – hence why it needs to be trained and tapped into even further.

3. *The Power of Ambition* by Jim Rohn

Ambition will drive you forward and ambition will get you to where you need to go. Having a very strong ambition will fuel your inner desire to succeed. If you do not have ambition, then you will not get very far.

Jim has a rather direct style of writing which is fantastic. Many books you read will beat about the bush and provide a lot of fluff but not a lot of content. *The Power of Ambition* delivers punch after punch after punch of good, strong and informative content.

The more ambition you have and the more you strive for success, then the greater the chances of it happening.

4. *The Magic of Thinking Big* by David J. Schwartz

Thinking big will lead you to big things. You can achieve anything and everything in your life if you are thinking big enough. If you think small then you limit your mind, your abilities and your thoughts. Thinking big opens up a whole new world of opportunities.

This book has some very useful content and strategies for helping you to think big. The sheer simplicity of the content is why it has been recommended.

5. *How to Win Friends & Influence People* by Dale Carnegie

Managing relationships in one way or another is the key to winning friends and influencing people. The language we use, the way we say it, the way we do things, the way we act and do not act, are all integral parts of this masterclass of a book by Dale Carnegie. A very successful man in his day, you will find this book incredibly insightful.

It is definitely one of my favourites as it encourages you to show more empathy, sympathy and gets you to almost become a wordsmith when dealing with people. This is something that I actively enjoy doing as it is amazing to gauge the reactions of others when you place the emphasis on them rather than you with lines such as 'I want, I need, I think,' etc.

6. *Think and Grow Rich* by Napoleon Hill

This book is an evergreen and timeless classic. How is it even possible to think and grow rich? Napoleon Hill reveals this secret in depth and really gets your mind thinking of how to do it. Released in 1937, this book has stood the test of time and is one of the most read business and mindset books on the planet.

Personally, I found this book difficult to read and to listen to. However, that does not take away from the fact that there are some very valuable life lessons nestled away in the text, hence its recommendation.

7. *Can't Hurt Me* by David Goggins

This book is ridiculously powerful. If you thought that you had a tough life, then David Goggins will blow you away with his story. From broken marriages to extreme training conditions and putting his body through unbelievable challenges, *Can't Hurt Me* really demonstrates that the mind is a powerful tool (probably the most powerful tool that we have). This book also demonstrates that you really can achieve anything that you set your mind to do.

What To Do Next

These seven books have been highly influential and hold great power within. Whatever we do in life is really down to us. We can achieve what we want to, especially if we believe it in our own minds. Taking action and thinking on an astronomical scale will help you.

The best part is being able to read them over and over again, making notes and then taking consistent action.

Your action point is to buy them and read them. If you have already read them, then read them again, take notes and take action.

Introduction To Property

Cheers!

We have reached the property part of this book. I can almost hear that sigh of relief that you have just let out. We will deep dive into buying property, how to do it, what not to do, where to buy, where not to buy and so much more.

First of all though, why invest in property in the first place? You have covered your 'whys' and goals already, which is fantastic, yet there are very practical reasons why you should invest in bricks and mortar.

Why Invest In Property?

Advantages

Why would you not want to invest in property? That is probably the more appropriate question. There are numerous advantages of investing in property. In a nutshell though:

1. Property provides a solid investment as property should (done correctly) enable a positive cashflow per month which would mean that you have invested in a positive cash-flowing asset.

2. If you were to work out the gross yield and the net return on investment (NET ROI) then you will more than likely find that the rates would be higher than having money sitting in the bank.

3. When inflation is higher than the interest rate, then your money that is sitting in the bank is effectively eroding away. Why would you let this happen to you? Why would you let this happen to your money? Your savings that you have worked hard for will, over time, be eroded away naturally and your purchasing power will decrease over time. So many people do not realise this.

For example, if you have a gross yield on a property that is 10% per annum and inflation is 2.5% per annum then you are technically earning 7.5% per annum.

You may as well get your money working for you rather than you working for your money. This key concept alone has helped many with the property investor mindset shift.

Disadvantages

Can things in property go wrong? Yes, is the simple answer. Things can go wrong. Will they go wrong? Not if you do your due diligence and take the necessary action.

Things that could go wrong include:

1. You may not get any tenants; you may get horror tenants that trash your property; you may get a hole in the roof which needs repairing; or you may have someone that decides to use the property for a cannabis farm. Your house could also be hit by lightning, taken over my aliens or just fall apart randomly!

2. Interest rates could also go up which means that your cashflow can decrease.

3. House prices can easily fall which means that your property could be worth less when it comes around to refinancing it.

4. You might get overcharged for renovations (for example, you might get ripped off).

The point is that, yes, things can go wrong in property and things will inevitably go wrong in property, but that is part of the fun. It is also a good reason as to why you should not just rely on one property and should have multiple properties.

Don't let the above reasons put you off investing at all. Do not let your fear take over. You have to be able to ride the rough with the smooth, hence the mindset book recommendations earlier on!

What is Buy-to-Let?

Buy-to-let is a British term that refers to buying a property with the specific intention to let out that property.

How does Buy-to-Let work?

You buy a property, renovate the property (if necessary) to add value and then rent the property. Ideally, your rental income will be enough to pay for the mortgage and other expenses and leave you in positive cashflow at the end of each month.

The idea is that you purchase the property below market value (BMV), add value to the property, and then re-mortgage the property in order to draw out your original capital investment.

As you will discover, there is much more to property than meets the eye.

Is Buy-to-Let for You?

This is where that big dose of reality comes in.

Buy-to-let is not for everyone. Buy-to-let isn't a particularly 'sexy' property investment strategy because it is not necessarily quick in terms of reaching financial freedom.

If financial freedom is something that you need to achieve VERY quickly then buy-to-let will probably not be for you.

From experience, the buy-to-let model provides a very good and solid foundation from which you can build your portfolio and gain a lot of good property knowledge at the same time.

You will learn many lessons from doing the basics on the most simple property model available.

If you are looking to steadily grow your portfolio and to have a solid foundation, then buy-to-let is definitely for you.

Economics of Buy-to-Let and the 18-Year Property Cycle

Property is a long-term business. Property success does not just happen overnight and there are economic factors behind property that will determine when you should buy and sell and when you should not buy and not sell.

There is an 18-year property cycle that exists.

For those of you fortunate (or unfortunate) enough to remember, the last two big economic recessions in the UK were between 1990-1992 and then between 2007-2008.

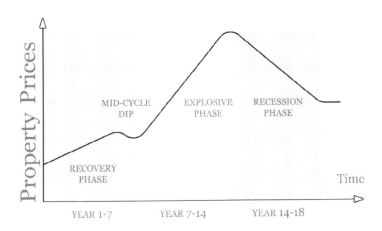

The rule of thumb is that after a recession, the market will enter a recovery phase which lasts 1–7 years. Traditionally there will be a mid-cycle wobble, which will be followed by an explosive stage in the market. This normally lasts between years 7–14 of the cycle.

Years 14–18 of the cycle typically involves four years of decline in the market before the cycle starts all over again.

Between years 13–14 of the cycle is where you do not want to be buying properties. This is because the prices will be inflated and because a recession is more than likely to be around the corner, thus reducing prices.

Think about where we are at the moment. At the time of writing (and at the time of production) the magical word that is Brexit is consuming the UK one way or another. Brexit is coinciding with a mid-market wobble, albeit a little bit later than normal in terms of the 18-year cycle.

Once Brexit has subsided one way or another, then the economy will more than likely take an upward trajectory before heading into a recession. This will probably be between 2025–2027 and that is just based on recent cycles. It may come earlier or it may come later. The thing is that it WILL come at some point.

We'd all be incredibly naïve to think that it will not happen. What eventually causes the next big recession is anyone's guess. I believe it will be some form of pension crisis.

Understanding this market cycle is fundamental to you as a property investor as it will help you to assess when to buy, when not to buy, when to sell (if that is a strategy that you choose to adopt) and when not to sell.

Investment mechanisms – LLP, Sole Trader, Ltd Company

There are many different ways in which you can purchase your properties. You could purchase them in your own name, in joint names (eg. with your spouse), as a Limited Liability Partnership or as a Limited Company.

How you go about purchasing your properties is completely up to you and it is highly recommended that you take professional advice from an accountant, tax planner and your mortgage broker. These will be covered in more depth in the Power Team section.

Cash vs. Mortgage

For the purposes of this book, we will assume that you will be buying your properties with either cash or a mortgage (whether that is as an individual, LLP or as Ltd company).

What is a mortgage?

I love history, so here is some historical background on the word "mortgage".

Mortgage is a 14th Century French word derived from the Latin word 'mori' which means to die.

Mortgage quite literally means "death pledge". Mort = "death" and gage = "pledge".

This might sound incredibly scary, but it is not.

It is called a mortgage because it means that the deal dies either when the debt is paid or when payment fails.

This makes perfect sense. As a sensible buy-to-let investor, you will always make sure that you pay your mortgages on time so you really have nothing to fear.

Different Types of Mortgages

There are many different types of mortgages that you can have. As with anything in this book, it is highly recommended that you speak to a qualified mortgage broker as they will be able to help you with your mortgage requirements. A good mortgage broker will be worth their weight in gold.

I am not a mortgage broker, independent financial advisor or FCA regulated, so can only suggest that you look to use interest-only mortgages for your property portfolio (and, quite possibly, your own home too) due to the fact that inflation will naturally erode the debt of the mortgage over time, thus creating more equity within your portfolio due to the increase in house prices due to inflation.

There are two main types of mortgages that you can have:

Capital and Repayment Mortgage

A repayment mortgage is a term generally used in the UK to describe a mortgage in which the monthly repayments consist of repaying the capital amount borrowed as well as the accrued interest. Overall, the amount that is borrowed decreases as time goes on and the loan would have been fully repaid at the end of the term.

For example, if you had a mortgage payment term of 25 years and had £100,000 on that mortgage, after 25 years of paying that mortgage you would have no mortgage left to pay.

Interest-Only Mortgage

An interest-only mortgage is a mortgage where the borrower pays only the interest for some or all of the term, with the principle balance unchanged during the interest-only period. At the end of the interest-only term, the borrower must renegotiate another interest-only mortgage or pay the sum outstanding.

For example, if you had a mortgage payment term of 25 years and had £100,000 on that mortgage, after 25 years of paying ONLY the interest on that mortgage, you would still have £100,000 at the end of the term.

This can seem quite scary, yet inflation should push up the price of your property and erode away the interest-only debt as a result, thus giving you more equity in your portfolio.

Once you have decided on what mortgage type you are going for, then you will have to decide whether or not you want a fixed rate or a variable/tracker rate. (Again, get your broker to explain this to you if you do not already know.)

Fixed Interest Rate Mortgage

A fixed-rate mortgage occurs where the interest rate on the mortgage remains the same through the term of the loan, as opposed to loans where the interest rate may adjust or vary (i.e. tracker/variable rate mortgages).

The key advantages for fixed interest rate mortgages are that you will know your monthly payments (as they will remain constant throughout) and you will be able to budget accordingly without having a fear that interest rates will rise and that your mortgage payments will rise as a result.

Tracker/Variable Mortgage Rates

A variable-rate mortgage, or tracker mortgage, is a mortgage where the interest rate on the mortgage is periodically adjusted based on an index which reflects the cost to the lender of borrowing on the credit markets. In the UK, this rate is referred to as the LIBOR rate.

The variable-rate mortgage/tracker mortgage may be offered at the lender's standard variable rate/base rate. There may be a direct and legally-defined link to the underlying index, but where the lender offers no specific link to the underlying market or index, the rate can be changed at the lender's discretion

Mortgage Summary

There are advantages and disadvantages to taking out each type of mortgage and this will depend on your risk tolerance and your plans for your portfolio moving forward.

Speak to a mortgage broker about your mortgage options.

Buying With Cash

The one simple advantage of being a cash buyer is that you will be able to purchase a property much faster than via a mortgage.

You will also not necessarily need to get searches done when buying with cash, although it is always recommended to do so for best practice.

There will be times where it is necessary to purchase a property in cash. Examples include:

- The seller needs a quick sale and only cash will do.
- The property is not mortgageable (i.e. no kitchen, structural defects).
- When the deal is that good and cash will get the deal done quicker than a mortgage.

Cash is king when it comes to purchasing property.

When a property is bought with cash, then, as a general rule of thumb it becomes easier for that property to be refinanced. This is assuming that there are no major structural issues with the property.

Buying With A Mortgage

Buying with a mortgage takes more time, searches are required (although you can get search liability insurance instead) and there is more paperwork involved when buying with a mortgage.

A mortgage broker will do the donkey work for you. They will find the right mortgage product for you, fill out a lot of the paperwork and will (with luck) see the mortgage offer through to completion. A good broker will have a decent client base, will always be busy but careful not to overstretch themselves, will have a good eye to detail, and will have good, solid relationships with mortgage lenders.

Buying with a mortgage does mean that you are able to leverage the bank's money as well. This means that you will be able to make your money work harder for you, as you will be leaving less money in a property.

Cash vs. Mortgage

There are a couple of tables that demonstrate the differences between buying with cash and buying with a mortgage. You will note for the purpose of these examples that:

- Legals have been set at £1,300 (this will vary depending on the purchase price of the property and how much your solicitor will charge for the conveyancing);
- The finance and survey costs have been set at £500 (this will vary depending on if you have a survey done on the property and how much your broker charges as well);
- The refinance and legals have been set at £2,000 (this will vary depending on how much your broker charges you and how much your solicitor charges you for the conveyancing);
- An assumption has been made that the property does not need any work doing to it;

- An assumption has been made that you are not using a sourcing agent to buy this property;
- Stamp Duty Land Tax is £2,400. This is correct for an £80,000 purchase yet please note that this will vary depending on the purchase prices of your properties;
- When buying with cash it is not a requirement that you have to get searches done – this helps to speed up the buying process.

Stamp Duty Land Tax

SDLT is applicable if you buy a property or land over a certain price in England and Northern Ireland.

In Wales it is called Land Transaction Tax and in Scotland it is called the Land and Buildings Transaction Tax.

You can find numerous SDLT calculators online which will help you to determine how much SDLT you will need to pay per property.

SDLT varies depending on what type of property you are buying (i.e. mixed use and commercial is charged differently from residential).

Thanks to the infinite wisdom of the government, buyers of second homes (whether they be buy-to-let or holiday homes) have to pay a 3% surcharge over the standard rate of SDLT. This came into effect in April 2016 and while many people grumbled, it just creates more opportunities for you and I because it puts off others from entering the market in the first place.

The example below shows the difference in net return on investment (NET ROI) if you buy an £80,000 property for cash or with a mortgage.

For the purpose of this example, it is assumed that the monthly rent is £650, that you will put 10% of gross rent aside per month for monthly operating expenses (MOE), that management for the property is 10% and that your mortgage rate is 4% per annum.

Cash					
Purchase Price:	£ 80,000		Monthly Rent		£ 650
Works Budget:	£ -		Annual Gross Rent		£ 7,800
Source Fee:	£ -		Management		£ 780
Legal Fees:	£ 1,300		MOE		£ 780
Finance & Survey Costs:	£ 500				
Stamp Duty Land Tax	£ 2,400				
Refinance Costs + Legals	£ 2,000				
Total Investment:	£ 86,200		Net Rent:		£ 6,240
			Monthly Net Rent:		£ 520
Mortgage LTV:	0%				
Mortgage Amount	£ -		Interest Rate:		0.00%
			Annual Mortgage Cost:		£ -
Deposit Amount	£ 80,000		Monthly Mortgage Cost:		£ -
			Monthly Cashflow:		£ 520.00
			Yearly Cashflow:		£ 6,240.00
Gross Yield	9.75%				
NET ROI on Cash Left In Deal:	7.80%				

With Mortgage					
Purchase Price:	£ 80,000		Monthly Rent		£ 650
Works Budget:	£ -		Annual Gross Rent		£ 7,800
Source Fee:	£ -		Management		£ 780
Legal Fees:	£ 1,300		MOE		£ 780
Finance & Survey Costs:	£ 500				
Stamp Duty Land Tax	£ 2,400				
Refinance Costs + Legals	£ 2,000				
Total Investment:	£ 86,200		Net Rent:		£ 6,240
Total Investment with Deposit	£ 26,200		Monthly Net Rent:		£ 520
Mortgage LTV:	75%				

With Mortgage				
Mortgage Amount	£ 60,000		Interest Rate:	4.00%
			Annual Mortgage Cost:	£ 2,400.00
Deposit Amount	£ 20,000		Monthly Mortgage Cost:	£ 200.00
			Monthly Cashflow:	£ 320.00
			Yearly Cashflow:	£ 3,840.00
Gross Yield		9.75%		
NET ROI on Cash Left In Deal:		19.20%		

You can see from this example that the Gross Yield is the same. That is correct, as Gross Yield simply is Annual Gross Rent divided by the Purchase Price. That will not change, whether the property was purchased with cash or with a mortgage.

However, the Net ROI jumps from 7.80% with cash, to 19.20% when with a mortgage. This is because you are leveraging the bank's monies. Yes, the cashflow has gone down from £520 to £320, yet your return is higher.

Leverage is such an important word in property and when used to its maximum potential, it will benefit you immensely.

If you had £80,000 sitting in the bank and you put all of that into buying one property, then your cashflow would be £520 per month and you would have a portfolio worth £80,000.

If you used that same £80,000 but purchased three identical properties (all with mortgages), then your cashflow would increase to £960 per month (3 x £320) AND you would also have a portfolio worth £240,000.

See how that same capital investment can yield two completely different results.

Cash Capital Pot	Mortgage Capital Pot
£80,000	£80,000
Asset Base (1 x £80,000)	3 x £80,000
£80,000	£240,000
Cashflow (1 x property)	3 x properties
£520	£960
Mortgage Debt	Mortgage Debt
£0	£180,000.00
Equity	Equity
£80,000.00	£60,000.00

Summary

There will be times where buying with cash will be much more advantageous. Cash enables you to be able to buy faster, is generally less hassle than buying with a mortgage and will give you an unencumbered asset. Sometimes a property is not mortgageable and therefore cash is the answer. You may also have religious beliefs that mean that you are not able to take out a mortgage due to the interest rates. This is because of beliefs that interest should never be charged on loans or that people should benefit from interest on loans.

For example, a Muslim is not allowed to benefit from lending money or receiving money from someone. This means that earning interest (riba) is not allowed – whether you are an individual or a bank. To comply with these rules, interest is not paid on Islamic savings or current accounts, or charged on Islamic mortgages.

When and where possible, religious beliefs permitting, buying with a mortgage is much more suitable as you will be able to leverage the money from the bank in order to increase your asset base and asset worth. This also means that you will not be putting all of your eggs in one basket.

Power Teams

In order to help you to become a successful property investor, you will need a power team.

What is a Power Team?

A power team is a term that you will hear quite a lot in property. Aristotle got the idea of a power team spot on when he coined the phrase: *'The whole is more than the sum of its parts.'* Aristotle wasn't necessarily talking or thinking about buying property, but the phrase certainly has stood the test of time.

Why Do You Need A Property Power Team?

Can you imagine trying to take over every single aspect of a property – buying, renovating, lettings, dealing with tenants, dealing with mortgage companies, etc?

You would have to go to law school and train to become a conveyancer; you would have to have to be very good at DIY in order to be able to renovate a property; you would have to be fairly good at advertising and marketing in order to first buy the property and then to let the property out.

Why would you want to go through all of this pain, hassle and stress when you can just pay for someone else's expertise?

By having a team of professionals around you and by constantly working with them, you will be able to get a lot more done in your time – such as viewing properties, building your business, etc.

A power team will help you get to where you want to go a lot quicker than if you were to undertake every single aspect yourself.

How Do You Find Your Power Team?

The Internet, social media and personal recommendations are the best ways to find your property power team. Builders will be local to your area, and so too will an estate agent and lettings agent. Your local mortgage valuer or surveyor will ideally have a very good knowledge and understanding of your investment area, but this is not always the case.

Your solicitor and accountant do not have to be local to your property investing area but should have an extensive knowledge of property and ideally be property investors themselves.

At the moment, I live and invest primarily in Hull. My accountant and solicitor are in Hull, my mortgage broker is in London and my tax consultant is in Cheltenham. Most of my power team are based in Hull, but I do leverage other property sourcing agents (more on that later) and their power teams when and where possible.

Who Do You Need In Your Power Team?

This is a very common question and the answer is: it depends on your property investment strategy. For example, if you are buying a regular £70,000 buy-to-let property in Hull, then it is very unlikely that you will need an architect, planning consultant or a commercial agent.

Rather than over complicating the ideologies and various strategies and scenarios, I have compiled a list of the 14 people I believe that you need in your property power team.

14 PEOPLE YOU NEED IN YOUR PROPERTY POWER TEAM

1. Estate Agents

90% of deals go through estate agents. If an agent knows what you are looking for and you build a good relationship with them, then they can be a really useful source of deals for you. In my experience, it is better to work with the smaller independent agents rather than the bigger chains. Estate agents may seem scary, but in truth they are not. They will always have a good source of deals because they are dealing with property and vendors day in and day out.

Prove that you are reliable and you may make it into the famed 'little black book' where you may get access to deals that do not even make it to the market.

It is always worth staying in touch and maintaining this relationship.

2. Commercial Agents

Like estate agents, commercial agents can be an incredibly useful source of deals – especially if you are looking at commercial conversions or land developments. If you are looking at regular buy-to-lets, then a commercial agent is not likely to be of much use. However, sometimes they do get residential properties appearing on their books, so it is always worth having a look and a chat every now and then.

Commercial agents can be easier to work with as they have a better understanding of how deals are structured and are more flexible than many high street estate agents.

As with estate agents, you want to build up a good relationship and make it into their 'little black book'.

3. Lettings Agents

Unless you want to manage your own properties, then a lettings agent will be a key member of your power team. Lettings agents are also very good sources of information as they will know plenty of landlords. A good lettings agent will know what they are doing. Take time to build the relationship with them and ask them questions and understand their processes. After all, they will be managing your properties, so you will want to know that they know what they are doing.

4. Solicitor

A solicitor will help you to buy property by undertaking conveyancing and all the searches and legalities that come with it. For your standard bread and butter buy-to-lets and HMOs, you can use a normal conveyancer.

For larger projects or more complex property purchases or agreements (such as a lease option), you will want to use a specialist solicitor. This is because a normal conveyancer may not know of a lease option or how they work. Finding the right person for the job is crucial, especially as a specialist solicitor will be able to push the more complex deals forward.

Solicitors really are a case of trial and error. Some of them are very slow and painful to work with, whereas some are quick and efficient. Once you have a solicitor that you get on well with and who works diligently, then keep hold of them! They will be worth their weight in gold.

5. Builder

Your property will more than likely need a refurbishment and who better to use than a local builder. You will always want to try to get three quotes for the work.

The best builders come via word-of-mouth recommendation or by using a website such as checkatrade.com.

Some builders have reputations for being cowboys and we have all seen the horror stories in the news or on the television about people getting ripped off.

The easiest way to combat this is to know what you want in your property and to have a rough knowledge of trade prices for items such as kitchens, bathrooms and central heating systems, etc. A builder may be able to double up as a project manager and will therefore be able to sub-contract the various trades such as electricians and plumbers. Your builder may be an all-in-one and may be able to do it themselves.

Never pay a builder 100% up-front. Ideally you should pay in stages, or pay on completion of a snagging list after the refurbishment has been completed. For the smaller refurbishments, I personally like to pay 50% up-front and then 50% on completion of a snagging list.

A snagging list is a list of the minor bits and pieces that need doing at the end of a refurbishment. For example, the painter and decorator might have got some gloss on the wall by accident so that will need correcting.

6. Architect

If you are looking at renovations, house extensions, commercial conversions, land developments or anything similar, then an architect is essential. They will be able to provide drawing and details of the projects, create workflow processes and even (sometimes) manage the build itself.

Architects are invaluable when it comes to this scale of work.

7. Planning Consultant

A good planning consultant will help you to get your projects through the quagmire that can be the planning system. If you are looking at commercial conversions, land, or changes of use then you will need to work with a planning consultant.

Some planning consultants also have very good links with council officers. This can sometimes be worked to your advantage, especially if you have multiple projects and developments you are looking to do and get through planning.

Always ask your planning consultant for a recommendation for an architect. If you have an architect and planning consultant that get on well with one another, then chances are that your project will run a lot smoother.

Your planning consultant needs to be local to your investment area as they will have an extensive knowledge of what the local council wants/doesn't want, etc.

8. Mortgage Valuer/Surveyor

A mortgage valuer/surveyor will be the ones that value your property. Nine times out of 10 your mortgage lender will pick your valuer and you will have no say in the matter.

Sometimes a valuer/surveyor will wake up on the wrong side of the bed and it doesn't matter what you do or say, your property is getting down-valued. This might not seem fair, but it is the nature of the beast.

Treat your valuer/surveyor with respect. Show up on time, be pleasant, smile and ask them about their jobs, their day. Some small talk may just be the difference between a bad valuation and a good valuation.

9. Mortgage Broker

Your mortgage broker is one of the most important people you will have on your team. Tell your broker everything – even the name of your pet! A mortgage broker will be able to pair you with the correct finance product for your purchase. They will have good relationships with the lenders and will be able to help you get the necessary funding where possible.

A broker can only work with what you give them, so you must tell them everything. This helps them when dealing with their lenders.

10. Commercial Mortgage Broker

A commercial broker will have access to development finance and bridging companies. A commercial broker will also have access to products for (surprise, surprise) commercial use such as shops, light industrial units and larger developments.

It is not necessary to use a commercial mortgage broker for just one regular buy-to-let property, but you may want to use one for HMO products and anything bigger.

Tell your broker everything. The better equipped they are, then the more they will be able to help you.

11. Property Accountant

Your property accountant will help you to set up your business. Your accountant should be able to do many activities such as payroll, general bookkeeping, etc.

Ideally, your accountant will be a property investor as well. It is not essential, but if they are then this only works in your favour as they will be taking care of their portfolios at the same time and will be up to date with regulations and changes to property legislation.

12. Property Tax Planner

If you are looking to scale your business and run multiple properties and businesses, then take advantage of the free one-hour sessions that property tax planners offer. Although your accountant may be good, they may not know everything about property tax. A specialist, such as a property tax planner, will; they will also be able to help you plan for the future. They will be able to help you structure your business(s) very effectively for the short, medium and long-term.

13. Property Sourcing Agent

If you live a long way from your investment area and struggle to find property, then you may want to consider using a property sourcing agent. As with anyone in your power team, it takes time to build up the relationship and credibility. Sourcing agents (as with builders) sometimes have reputations for being cowboys and money grabbers.

Take your time to find someone reliable, trustworthy and who you feel you can get on well with.

A good, reputable sourcing agent will find properties that suit your criteria and pass them over to you for a fee. It is their job to find properties for investors like you and to get paid for doing so.

Again, the relationship here is crucial because not every property is always a 'deal'. So you must know your area, know what you want and know the sourcing agent.

14. Insurance Broker

Insurance is very important in property. You will want to make sure that your property is fully insured and – if you have a limited company – that you have the correct company and directors' insurance in place too.

Insurance can be a minefield and it is important to work with an expert in this field.

When you have multiple properties, you will be able to get 'portfolio' insurance too.

But remember...

Relationships are the most important thing. It is important to be able to work hand in hand with members of your power team. Do not be like a bull in a china shop. You know what you want from your power team and they know what they want from you. Take your time to build the relationships over time as they will more than likely bear fruit when you least expect it.

For example, if you are known for being a pleasant person to deal with and a quick payer, then when you have an urgent purchase/renovation, etc., it is more than likely that your power team will want to work with you and put your purchase/renovation to the top of their priority list rather than argumentative and slow-paying Dave from down the road.

Property is a people business. It is all about the relationships.

Episode 12 of The Property Nomads Podcast goes in depth into Property Power Teams. You can subscribe to The Property Nomads Podcast for FREE. Find us on iTunes, Stitcher, Spotify or whatever platform you listen to your podcasts on.

iTunes – https://apple.co/2UdfXXY

Stitcher – https://bit.ly/2uC2RVr

Spotify – https://spoti.fi/2Wvxk3I

PICKING YOUR AREA (10-5-2-1 MODEL)

Finding the best area to invest in!

The key to kickstarting your property investment career is to find the right area.

Assuming that cashflow and financial freedom are what you are after, then you should be aiming to invest in an area that produces properties that can make you at least £200 per month after all expenses (i.e. net profit).

Many people look at gross yield, but to me that is completely amateur.

Gross yield is not really a fair and accurate indication of the investment potential of a property at all as it does not take into account mortgage expenses, void periods, MOE and any other possible expenses.

You either invest for cashflow or capital growth (or a blend).

A general rule of thumb is that if you are investing for cashflow, then you will go to the North, certain parts of the Midlands and anywhere west of Bristol (eg. South Wales). Areas for capital growth generally include London, the South East and East Anglia.

There is no right and wrong in terms of investment areas. As long as your area has the key fundamentals – such as good transport connections, good schools and good work opportunities, – then you will be fine. That town or city could be Leicester, Middlesbrough, Sunderland, Grimsby, Newport (Gwent), Swansea, Bradford, Carlisle and many other towns and cities!

In a complete nutshell, the best area for you to invest in is the area where the numbers work, an area that you have done necessary due diligence on, an area that you feel comfortable investing in and an area that meets your investing needs.

HOW TO PICK YOUR AREA USING THE 10–5–2–1 MODEL

Your 10 Initial Areas

So far, you have established your 'why', your goals and that you want to invest in buy-to-let property for cashflow purposes.

You have established that for cash-flowing buy-to-let properties, you will go to the North, certain parts of the Midlands and anywhere west of Bristol (i.e. South Wales).

The 10–5–2–1 model is designed so that you are able to obtain your investment area in a sensible step-by-step process. Most of this can be done on your computer, so you can do this from the comfort of your own home!

Any area that you invest in should have strong fundamentals. The two sets of fundamentals that you will need to look out for are:

1.   Transport links (road, rail, airports, seaports, etc.)
2.   Industry (local employment, jobs, etc.)

Let's have a look at these two fundamentals on a one-by-one basis.

Transport Links (Road, Rail, Seaports, etc.)

Transport links are crucial. The towns and cities that you look at ideally will be located near a motorway or on a major 'A' road such as the A1. They will ideally have a railway station and should have decent links to an airport/airports, good bus links and good links to ports where necessary.

For example, let's take Newcastle upon Tyne. When you research Newcastle, you will see that it is in the North East region of England, has an airport, a railway station, a large hospital and (judging by the size of the area) a decent-sized population. It is also situated on the River Tyne and is close to another city, Sunderland.

(The image below shows how close Newcastle is to Sunderland)

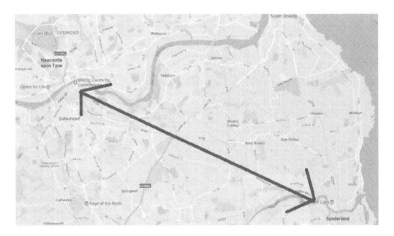

If you were to look at King's Lynn in Norfolk, you will see that it is not quite the same size as Newcastle. It does have a railway station, it is not really near any other major towns or cities, but does have ok road connections that go west, east and south. In general, it is not as well-connected as Newcastle upon Tyne.

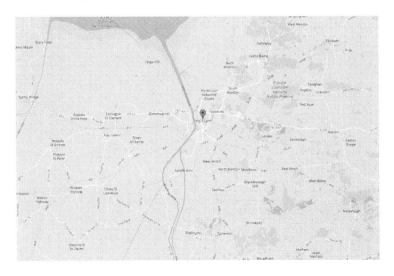

Industry (Local Employment, Jobs, etc.)

The easiest way to gain some quick knowledge of local industry is to use Wikipedia or Google. Using either will give you a decent understanding of the major employers in the area and a quick history about the area.

Take 10 minutes or so on each of your chosen 10 areas in order to get more information about its fundamentals and industry. Make your bullet points too.

Using Newcastle upon Tyne and King's Lynn as examples, we can find out the following about Newcastle:

- It is the main hub for the North East of England.
- It has a key central business district in the city centre.
- It boasts several major shopping centres.
- It has great rail connections with Scotland, London, Manchester, Liverpool, York and many more cities.
- It has an airport with very good international connections.
- It has very good road connections with the South and Scotland.
- The city has a population of approximately 290,000.

In comparison, King's Lynn has:

- A population of approximately 45,000.
- A good seaport.
- Good fishing and seafood industries.
- A decent rail connection with places such as London, Cambridge and Ely.
- Ok road connections. It can be quite time-consuming to drive to Peterborough and Norwich.
- No convenient airport nearby.

Just from some basic map and Wikipedia research, it is clear that Newcastle has more to offer than King's Lynn. This is not to disparage King's Lynn in any way, yet it is important to remember that buy-to-let works really well in areas where the population is higher and where there are good transport connections and demand for work.

King's Lynn is not in as good a location as Newcastle, and is quite far from the next biggest towns and cities (Peterborough, Cambridge and Norwich).

Newcastle is very close to Sunderland, has better transport connections and a much higher population. This works in its favour.

Take 10–15 minutes going through Google Maps and make a note of 10 places that you think have strong fundamentals. When you have selected your 10 areas, then make bullet-pointed notes on each area in order to compare them. Use local council websites or even Wikipedia to do some extra research. You may already be familiar with an area which is advantageous.

Once you have found your 10 places and have made some bullet-pointed notes, you are ready to eliminate five of them.

From 10 to 5

Now that you have chosen 10 areas and have made bullet-pointed notes about them, you are ready to whittle 10 down to five. The easiest thing to do is to create a quick tick box for your 10 areas.

This is an exact replica of the table that I used in the past, so it is highly recommended that you just copy it.

Area	Railway station?	Airport (within an hour)	Motorways	Tourist Attractions	Docks	University	Hospital

Write your areas in the left-hand column, each on its own row.

What you need to do now is to fill out each of the 10 areas to see if they have any of the seven key indicators. Put a Y in the box if your area does and leave the box blank if your area does not.

Area	Railway station?	Airport (within an hour)	Motorways	Tourist Attractions	Docks	University	Hospital
Newcastle	Y	Y	Y	Y	Y	Y	Y
King's Lynn	Y			Y	Y		

You'll see from the above diagram that Newcastle upon Tyne ticks all of the boxes whereas King's Lynn only has a railway station, some tourist attractions and docks.

After you have completed the task, you will have different levels of Y's for your different areas.

Add up and total the Y's for each area.

The five areas with the fewest Y's can be disregarded.

The five areas with the highest number of Y's will be the five areas that you look at next.

If you have a tie of Y's for your chosen areas, then look back at your bullet-pointed notes and make a personal gut instinct judgement call in order to eliminate a town/city.

From 5 to 2

Now, you have five areas to choose from. This is a great start. The next step is to do some more in-depth desktop research, but this time to actually look at various areas within your five current towns/cities.

For this, you will need to visit www.mouseprice.com and click on Heatmaps (on the bottom right) as seen in the diagram below.

The heatmap system will be able to help you to pinpoint areas and average house prices. Type in one of your current five places and click on search.

You will now see a colour-coded heatmap of your area. Back in the day, Mouseprice used to have the colours linked to how much the properties were worth (i.e. maroon would indicate houses worth more than £500,000), but Mouseprice have now got rid of this. It is a little inconvenient, but do not worry, I have listed the colours in order. This shows the cheapest to most expensive areas by colour:

- Dark Blue.
- Medium Blue.
- Light Blue.
- Turquoise.
- Green.
- Light Green.
- Yellow.
- Amber.
- Light Red.
- Blood Red.
- Maroon.

The general rule of thumb is that the Light Blue/Turquoise areas tend to be better areas to look at. I stress that this is not conclusive, but a general rule of thumb. Local area knowledge will always trump computer data. (If you are reading the paperback, go to www.mouseprice.com to see an accurate representation of the colours.)

You will see the turquoise areas in Newcastle upon Tyne as shown on the Heatmap.

Once you have located two different turquoise areas within your five towns/cities, then you will need to go onto Rightmove.

Your turquoise areas could be:

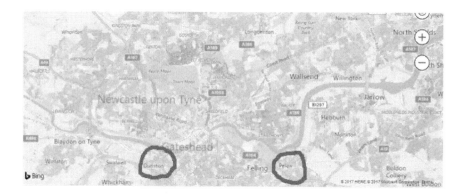

On Rightmove, you will need to locate the same areas as you have found on mouseprice.com.

Using Rightmove, search for properties that are For Sale and that have a minimum of two bedrooms.

For Dunston – some examples are above.

Using the same area, and still using Rightmove, go onto the For Rent section and make notes of the prices.

Once you have done this, then multiply the average rental by 12, divide this number by the average For Sale price and multiply by 100. This will give you basic gross yield figures.

Make sure that the rental is for a For Sale property of the same specification. (In the example, the rents are for two-bed flats and the flats for sale are two-bed flats.)

From this example in Dunston, you will see that gross yield will be 7.71%.

12 x £450 (rent per month) = £5,400 (annual rent).

£5,400 (annual rent)/£70,000 (purchase price) x 100 = 7.71%

However, gross yield is an amateur way of looking at investments in property, so you will need to take this a step further.

The next thing to do would be to go onto an online mortgage calculator. If you type the words "online mortgage calculator" into your internet browser, then one should appear automatically. If not, then use: https://www.moneysavingexpert.com/mortgages/mortgage-rate-calculator

Let's assume that you will be buying the property with a mortgage.

Let's also assume that you will be buying using a 25% deposit (so a 75% Loan-to-Value Mortgage).

If the assumed purchase price is £70,000, then the deposit will be £17,500 (£70,000/100 x 25).

Your mortgage (as a result) will be £52,500.

At the time of writing, interest rates are very favourable due to economic circumstances. However, any professional should stress-test mortgage interest rates. For the purpose of working through this example, stress-test the interest rate at 5%.

Mortgage calculator

Monthly cost		Maximum loan
Mortgage amount	Interest rate (%)	Mortgage period (years)
£ 52,500	5	25

Total cost of mortgage	£92,073
Monthly payments	£307

You will see that the online mortgage calculator states that the mortgage for this property will be £307 per month based on a £52,500 mortgage with an interest rate of 5%. It is more than likely that your interest rate will be lower than 5%, yet it is better to stress-test and be safe rather than sorry.

Your cashflow (before management expenses and MOE) will be £143 (£450 – £307).

Your cashflow (after management expenses and MOE, and assuming that management and MOE are 10% of gross monthly rent) will be £53 (£450 – £307 – £45 (management fee) – £45 (MOE)).

Do the same numbers but also with the current limited company mortgage rates. (At the time of writing, they are approximately 3.5% – but check these with your mortgage broker first, as they could be higher or lower depending on when you are reading this and doing this exercise!)

Do the same exercise for the two turquoise areas that you have selected in each of your five chosen towns/cities. Put all of the results into a spreadsheet.

You should see instantly that the yields will differ, but more importantly that the potential monthly income will differ as well. Some will probably be quite low and some will probably be quite high.

Pick the two towns/cities that have the areas which are likely to provide you with the highest cashflow.

Congratulations – you have just whittled your five areas down to two.

Four Online Tools That Will Help You To Search For The Right Investment Properties

1. Rightmove

Rightmove should be a staple in your life if you are looking to invest in property. So much research and knowledge can be done from the comfort of your own home nowadays. Rightmove is the number 1 online vehicle for properties.

Rightmove is very simple to use. You use their very easy search criteria and a list of houses will come up depending on the criteria that you enter.

2. Zoopla

In my opinion, Zoopla has one advantage over Rightmove and that is the fact that you can view houses in your prospective area by selecting "highest discount" from the dropdown menu in the search bar. This is great as you will be able to at least see what properties have been reduced the most. However, having used both Zoopla and Rightmove extensively over the years for research, I will say that I prefer to use Rightmove.

3. OnTheMarket

OnTheMarket is just another online portal that you can view properties on.

It has to be noted that some independent estate agents will not use Rightmove and sometimes can therefore only be found on OnTheMarket.com.

4. Truffull

Truffull is an up-and-coming property search portal. Check it out at: www.truffull.co.uk.

Truffull is well laid out, simple to use and it is very easy to find a range of both residential and commercial property throughout the UK. At the moment, it is not as extensive as OnTheMarket, Zoopla or Rightmove, yet a lot of investors will not know about Truffull, so use this book and this advice and turn it into your competitive advantage within your area!

From 2 to 1

You are left with two potential areas. Now, you have to make a decision as to which one to choose to invest in.

Ideally, what you will want to do is to have an overnight stay in your two areas. Walk the streets, walk around the centre, get a feel for the area. Drive the streets throughout the day, drive the streets at night as well. Get a sense of as much as you can.

Keep an eye out for construction sites. Visit the local bus and train station. See what transport connections there are and where you can get to.

Instinctively, you will get a feel for the area; you will get good vibes or bad vibes.

If you are looking to work closely within your local area, then at least liking it will help.

If you don't mentally like your area then you will find that you will make excuses NOT to visit, NOT to look at properties, NOT to make offers and NOT to invest.

This may come across as being incredibly minor, but it can have a massive impact on everything moving forward.

Do this for both areas and make notes. Then, from all the information that you have compiled, and from visiting the two areas, you should know which area you are going to invest in.

If you are really undecided, then flip a coin.

Nine times out of ten, just visiting and area will help you to make up your mind. This is because you may get a feel for the area and not like it or for whatever other reason!

Go and stay in your areas, write up a pros and cons list, make an in-depth comparison between the two and pick one.

When I did this task, it came down to Liverpool and Hull. The numbers were better in Liverpool, but there was something more attractive about Hull at the time. I had a better vibe from the people I spoke to. My gut instinct told me to go with Hull and I've not looked back since.

Your Chosen Area

You have now got your area that you want to invest in! This is superb and congratulations. This is a big achievement as so many people get stuck in 'analysis paralysis' and never take the next step.

The key thing now is to re-visit your new area. Drive up for the day or spend a couple more days or nights there.

Buy a map of the local area, research the local estate and lettings agents and visit them.

The aim of this will be to really pinpoint the areas in which you want to buy your houses.

Take your map to a local lettings agent first and have a chat. You are there to find out what properties and property types are renting quickly, what the demand is for and where the demand is. You also want to know the places to avoid buying and where the demand for rentals is slow.

Ideally, you will get the local lettings agent to circle these areas on the map.

Don't just rely on one lettings agent. Go and repeat this with at least three and use a different map each time so that you can compare at the end of the day.

You will find that some agents will be more willing to help you than others.

From experience, it is better to chat to the independent lettings agencies as they seem to have a more hands-on approach and a more in-depth knowledge of the area rather than your bigger hybrid estate and lettings agents such as Reeds Rains Ltd, William H Brown, etc.

Once you have compiled the information about the areas, then you will have a much better understanding of the types of properties that are moving fast.

For example, "there is really high demand in Robert Street and Peter Street for two- and three-bed mid-terraced properties" or "four-bed houses on Dave Street are on the market for less than a week before being rented."

These basic examples will give you a fantastic understanding of the area. Always get at least three opinions. Sometimes what a lettings agent thinks is a good investment area doesn't necessarily mean that it is a good investment area.

The same can be said for rentals. Just because a few streets go well, it does not mean that the area is great for investment. For example, the four-bed houses on Dave Street may rent within seven days at £695 per month, but they are new-builds and cost £200,000 to buy.

After you have compiled this information from the lettings agents, then it is time to go around to the estate agents. Estate agents are an interesting bunch of people. You walk through the front door and nine times out of 10 you are met with a stare cold enough to even make an Eskimo shiver!

You are in a good situation though: you know what areas you are looking in and you know what streets you are looking for. Take the maps, show them the maps (don't tell them a lettings agent has done this) and say that you are after two- to three-bed properties on Robert Street and Peter Street.

You know that these properties are going to rent fast as there is a demand on those streets.

The lettings agents should have given you a good idea of a couple of different rows of streets (or areas) within your chosen area that work well for rental properties.

Normally, an estate agent will want to put you on their list of investors or their client list. This is fine and it is part of the game.

Go around the estate agents, introduce yourself and state what properties you are looking for and where you are looking for those properties.

Estate agents are a very good source of properties; most good investor properties do not even make it onto the market.

Play the game with estate agents – be nice, courteous and always look to create a win-win situation. Estate agents will help you and work with you because they like you.

In summary, your visit will result in you pinpointing areas within your chosen area. You will come away from your area knowing what properties you are looking to buy, what streets/areas to buy them in and having built up a rapport with local estate and lettings agents.

Recap

So you now have your area for investment. You even have certain streets and areas within your chosen area that you are able to focus on. This is great. You will know the rough prices of these properties because you have done your online research and have spoken to estate and lettings agents.

Now you know what you are after, the next stage will be to book some viewings with some local estate agents.

Getting To Know Your Area In Depth

As with many things in property, getting to know your area takes time. It does not happen overnight.

You could do what I done and move to your investment area. Moving to Hull for the purpose of investing in property has been the second-best decision that I have ever made in my life.

Just in case you are wondering, the best decision was to decide to go travelling. This was because it opened my eyes up to the world and helped to put life into perspective.

Moving to your investment area may not be for you, as you may not have the circumstances to do so. If this is the case, then do not worry as there are things that you can do to really get to know your area.

Six ways to truly get to know your area in depth are:

1. Drive around your area

Go for a drive in the day and then do the same at night. An area that may appear very good by daylight may not be so great at night. Your gut instinct will tell you whether or not an area is good.

2. Talk to the locals

Having a pleasant chat with the people on the street about the local area will really help. Local people are more than likely to have inside information and will be able to tell you things that even your estate or lettings agent may not. Examples may include really bad areas, specifically bad roads and what the area was like 15 years ago

3. Read the local area plan

Every council will have a local area plan or something similar. It can normally be found on the council website.

This is a fantastic document to read as it will provide you with the plans that the council have for your area for the future. This document will more than likely have sites that the council want to develop, what their vision is for the town/city, how much is likely to be invested and what they are hoping to achieve.

This information will be useful to you and you will be able to use this to your advantage as you will have an understanding of the future economics of the area.

4. Read the local newspaper

When in your local area, take the time to pick up the local newspaper and have a read through it. You can normally get a good indication of what an area is like by what is in the newspaper. You can also search online for old newspaper articles and information.

As with anything in life, the more you know, the better the position you will be in.

5. Talk to local estate agents and lettings agents

Talking to local estate and lettings agents will be very useful for you to establish your area. Asking the right questions and taking the time out of your day to have a friendly conversation with them will really help you to determine which areas are good and which areas are not so good.

6. Book in an investor day

Some people are short of time and do not want the hassle (nor have the time) to be able to do all of the extensive research necessary. Many experienced investors will offer investor days. Investor days will usually include site visits, being driven around the area with the good and bad areas shown, examples of deals, and introductions to members of the power team. Some investor days may even include a round table mastermind too.

This is a very good way to leverage your time as investing in an investor day will enable you to fast-track your knowledge of a specific area.

It is typical to see investor days offered from anywhere between £197 to £497.

This may seem like a lot of money, yet rest assured it is not: £497 is no different from investing into a one-day course and, if you do your research properly on the people running the days, then you should get value for money.

The Property Nomads have been able to help a lot of people with our Hull investor days. We have had clients from Hong Kong, China and New Zealand spend days with us and we have been able to source and manage properties for them as a result.

They have been able to tap into our knowledge, our power team and our expertise. As a result, their investment journeys have accelerated and they have started buying properties. An absolute win-win situation.

If you're thinking of investing in Hull, want to tap straight into the knowledge that The Property Nomads have, and would like a Hull Discovery Day then e-mail me at rob@thepropertynomads.com straight away!

Goldmine Areas – How To Find Them

A goldmine area is a specific area or street where you will end up buying property because of a number of factors such as strong fundamentals, a good supply of discounted property and very strong rental demand.

It is important to note that 'supply' and 'discount' is individual to you, as some people would consider a supply of 10 per year to be good and some would consider a supply of 100 per year to be good.

There are two main ways to find your goldmine area:

1. Talk to local estate and lettings agents

Talking to local estate and lettings agents will be very useful for you to establish your area.

Step-by-step instructions for finding your goldmine area through estate and lettings agents are:

- Buy a map of the local area.
- Find three local lettings agents.
- Walk into each lettings agent and ask, 'What is renting quickly (eg. three-bed mid-terraced) and in what area(s)? Please draw this on the map.'
- Visit three local estate agents with your drawn-on map.
- Ask for whatever the lettings agents say is renting quickly, show them the map and see if the estate agent has any properties in those areas.

It is important to note that many estate agencies will have lettings agencies attached to them. Do NOT use these dual agencies. You need to speak to three different estate agents and three different lettings agents.

It is definitely still worth driving around these areas both in the daytime and at night. This is because what the lettings agent and estate agents tell you may not be the right areas for you. The lettings agent may give you areas where they 'prefer' to rent houses as these are nicer areas. This doesn't mean that the numbers are going to be any good for you, so you have to make sure that you do extra due diligence.

Remember that your aim as a property investor is to purchase a house/flat where there are good fundamentals in an area with strong rental demand and where the numbers work for you.

2. Rightmove/Google Research

Online research is simple and cost-effective. You will be able to pinpoint a few areas by just using Rightmove and Google. Follow this step-by-step guide and see what you find:

Step 1

Open up three tabs on your internet browser.

Tab 1 – www.rightmove.co.uk
Tab 2 – www.rightmove.co.uk
Tab 3 – www.google.co.uk

Step 2

Go to tab 1

On the Rightmove homepage enter the name of the village/town/city where you have decided to invest and click 'For Sale'

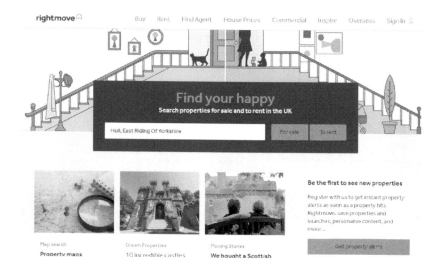

Step 3

The location should already be filled in.

Change the search radius to 'within 15 miles'.

Under Offer, Sold STC etc – tick this box.

Ignore all other boxes.

Click the 'Find Properties' button.

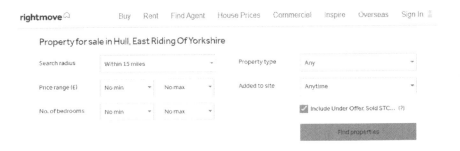

Step 4

At the top right of the page click on the 'Sort by – Lowest price first'.

Step 5

Scroll down and find the cheapest house or flat that is of regular construction i.e bricks.

Do not click on any commercial property, land or anything that is shared ownership.

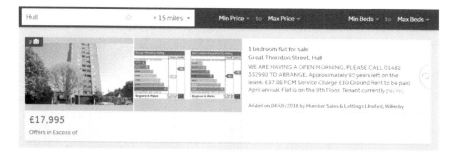

Step 6

Go to tab 3.

Type the street address that the property was on, town and postcode.

In this example: Huntingdon Street, Hull, postcode.

Click search and google will come up with a result for you.

Step 7

Go to tab 2 as it is time for you to find comparable properties.

Enter the new postcode that you have found in Step 6 and click on 'For Sale'.

You will need to use the following criteria:

- Search Radius – within ¼ mile.
- Property type – if your initial property was a house, then click "house". If a flat then click "flat".
- Number of bedrooms – same as the house you have found.
- Price range – no minimum and no maximum.

- Retirement properties – non-retirement only.
- Shared ownership – non-shared ownership.
- Added to site – any time.
- 'Under Offer, Sold STC etc' – tick this box.
- Click on 'Find Properties' button.

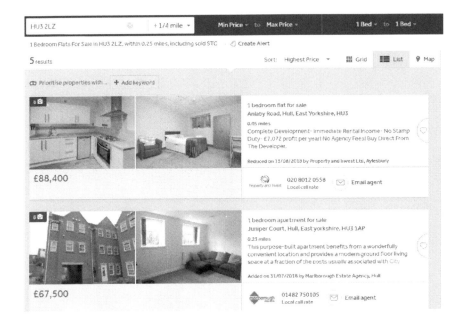

Step 8

The aim of this exercise is to find a similar property (size, bedrooms, style of property) but at a higher value. This will establish a good range of property and show you that there is a spread in the market.

The best comparables are going to be under offer or sold STC.

Step 9

If there is not a wide range of properties, then repeat Step 7 but change the following:

- Search radius – change to ½ mile.

The minute you get a 30% difference in prices between the lowest and the highest prices, then the chances are that you have found a goldmine area.

Summary

Being in your investment area and asking estate and lettings agents is a very good way of finding a goldmine area.

The best way to find your goldmine area is to combine advice from estate agents and lettings agents with doing in-depth desktop research.

Rightmove won't just give you properties and deals won't just jump out at you and fall in your lap. It is important to use this tool effectively and combine the other factors in this book too.

Types of Properties
You SHOULD Be Looking For

Once you have your goldmine areas, then you will need to go and look for properties.

The key thing to remember is that you are ideally looking for a property that is going to be below market value (BMV) and a property that you can add value to.

Adding value will typically mean refurbishing the property. For example, replacing/upgrading the kitchen, bathroom, painting and decorating, carpets, electrics, boiler system, etc.

When browsing through properties on Rightmove etc., you ideally do not want properties that are already 'done up'. Ninety-nine times out of one hundred, you need to be able to add value to your investment in order to justify the refinance value to the valuer (more on that later).

The only exception to this rule is when you know your area inside out. When you know your area inside out, then you'll be able to spot a bargain from a mile off.

For example, a property I purchased in one of my goldmine areas was available for £63,000. From local knowledge and knowing my area, I knew that that property was worth £80,000. No works were needed and it was already tenanted. Therefore, a purchase price of £63,000 on a property that should be worth £80,000 represents a discount of 22.85%. Not bad!

When you are refurbishing your property, you should be looking to add £3 of value for every £1 spent. In other words, £10,000 of works should aim to add £30,000 of value. This is a general rule of thumb and is not designed to be gospel.

Kitchens and bathrooms will generally add the most value to your property. So too will creating a new bedroom – for example, turning a two-bed property into a three-bed property. Yet this also depends on the floorplan and the area.

When searching for properties on Rightmove, you ideally want to be avoiding properties such as this one:

This is because they have already been done up. Unless they are discounted, then do not bother wasting the estate agent's time, or your own, with viewings.

Instead, you want to be arranging viewings for properties that need some work doing to them, such as this one:

You can see from the photos that the bathroom and kitchen are definitely in need of upgrading. The flooring could do with replacing too.

The best properties are ones where you only have one photo. Normally, there is only one photo for a reason. Any property like that should be worth viewing.

3 bedroom semi-detached house for sale   £130,000
Hillside, Gateshead, NE11

You can clearly see from this example that the property looks like an eyesore and that you will be easily able to add value externally by changing the guttering, front door and tidying up the garden. That's without checking out the inside.

Once you have browsed through Rightmove and Zoopla etc., then you need to go and view the properties.

Flats vs. Houses (Leasehold vs. Freehold)

A common debate that you will hear in property is: "Which is better, leasehold or freehold?"

When you are buying your investment properties, it is important to note that you will either be buying the freehold or the leasehold.

A general rule of thumb is that most flats are leasehold and most houses are freehold. There will be exceptions to this. For example, in Burnley, Lancashire, some houses are on a long leasehold rather than freehold.

What is a Leasehold?

A leasehold is a method of owning a property for a fixed term, but not necessarily the land that it sits on. Possession of a leasehold property is normally subject to ground rent and service charges being paid to the freeholder.

When the leasehold expires, then ownership of the property reverts back to the freeholder.

What is a Freehold?

A freehold is the outright ownership of property and the land that the property sits on. There are no time limits on the period of ownership.

Advantages of Leasehold

If you get a 'long leasehold' (eg. 900+ years), then this is pretty much as good as owning the freehold. Leaseholds, when granted, are often 90 or 120 years but can go as high as 999 years.

The maintenance of communal areas, the roof and the grounds will be the responsibility of the freeholder. Therefore, your maintenance bills could be lower.

I currently have a property in Burnley that is a two-bed mid-terrace that is on a long lease. I currently pay the freeholder a peppercorn rent (i.e. very minimal). At the time of writing, this equates to about £3 a year.

Get your solicitor to check out the terms of the lease as well (especially for modern flats in a modern block of apartments) as the service and maintenance charges can be quite high!

Disadvantages of Leasehold

Getting a mortgage could be a challenge, yet that will depend on the length of the lease.

Mortgage companies like to see at least a minimum of 75 years on the lease before they will consider lending. They will certainly want to see at least 50 years left on the lease at the end of the mortgage term.

If your lease has less than 75 years on it, then speak to your mortgage broker as they may have access to lenders that will lend on shorter leases.

Renewing a lease can be quite expensive. A lease can be renewed with the freeholder at a cost. This cost varies and, as a property investor, you will have to look at the investment value. For example, if your property makes £200 profit per month and your lease will cost £8,000 to renew, then it'll take 40 months for you to realise any profit again in that property.

As a leaseholder, you will more than likely have to pay ground rent, service charges and possibly some other charges to the freeholder.

Just remember to factor these in when doing your deal analysis.

Advantages of Freehold

With a freehold you have (within reason and within the parameters of the law) the ability and flexibility to do what you want and you don't necessarily need to ask anyone's permission to do anything.

NB – If you are looking to build on some land, or your property is in a conservation area, then you will need planning permission. Planning restrictions are tight if you are in a conservation area, so please make sure that you check with your local planning authority before conducting any changes or making any alterations.

As a freeholder you are in charge of your repairs, so if something goes wrong you can fix it straight away.

As a freeholder you are in charge of your own land, so you do not have any concerns with length of leases. The property is yours indefinitely.

As a freeholder you do not have to pay any ground rent or service charges or any other landlord charges.

Disadvantages of Freehold

Repairs are normally more expensive if you have a freehold property. For example, if the roof blows off or there is a leak, as a freeholder it is your responsibility to replace these items.

If your property falls into a state of disrepair, tenants are too noisy, or the rubbish is causing a nuisance to your neighbours, then you are legally and financially obliged to take the necessary action to remedy this.

Summary

If you are looking to buy flats in city centres because the rental demand is there and the fundamentals are strong, then that is great. Just make sure that you do your extra homework with regards to ground rent charges and service charges before committing. A good solicitor will be able to help you.

The same applies for freeholds: do your homework on your area, research properly and this will put you in a much better position moving forward.

What To Look For When Viewing A Property

As with anything in life, learning takes time and consistency. If you are reading this and are a seasoned investor or a builder, then viewing property may be a lot easier as you will be familiar with doing it.

You might be reading this and be thinking to yourself, 'That's okay Rob, but I have never viewed a property before in my life.' If you are thinking that, then think about it this way:

- Do you live in a house?
- Do you live in a flat?
- Do you live somewhere?

If the answer to any of those above questions is a yes, then chances are that you HAVE viewed a property before.

The 5 Things You MUST Look At When Viewing A Property

99% of us have the same challenges when it comes to viewing property. These challenges include: knowing what needs replacing, the price of individual parts and labour, and what the overall refurbishment cost is going to be.

Not knowing the refurbishment costs means that it is difficult to assess what offer you should put in on a property.

I remember when I first started viewing properties back in late 2015, I really had no idea what I was meant to be looking out for. I was just viewing properties because I knew that I had to do so in order to put offers in and to get offers accepted and to eventually create passive income and build an asset base.

1. Boiler/Central Heating System

Does the property have a boiler?

That seems like a completely obvious question, but some people do not check the simple items like this when viewing a property.

The property may instead have a giant water tank/water storage system or a hot air blowing system. This is not the end of the world, but having a modern combi boiler is very energy efficient and will be of benefit to both you and your tenants.

Remember to check if the property has a central heating system and radiators as well. If not, then chances are you will need to install a full heating system. Having a full heating system will keep your tenants and properties warm and will provide you with piece of mind.

Always check to see if the property you are viewing has a boiler and a radiator system.

If not, then you can expect to pay a couple of thousand pounds (at least) in order to purchase a heating system and to have it installed.

2. Electrics (consumer unit + plug sockets)

Electrics are a very important thing to look at when you are viewing a property. Key things to look out for are the fuse box/consumer units, earthing and plug sockets.

If the fuse box is really old, then you will need to upgrade it to a modern consumer unit. If the property already has a modern consumer unit in it, then that is great. (The Institution of Engineering and Technology defines a consumer unit as being *"a particular type of distribution board comprising a type-tested co-ordinated assembly for the control and distribution of electrical energy, principally in domestic premises, incorporating manual means of double-pole isolation on the incoming circuit(s) and an assembly of one or more fuses, circuit breakers, residual current-operated devices or signalling and other devices proven during the type-test of the assembly as suitable for use."*

I'm not an electrician but I know what one looks like!

An example of an old fuse box/consumer unit:

Earthing applies if there is an old fuse box. Some old properties do not have their electrics earthed, so when you upgrade your electrics you will need to install a new consumer unit and get the property 'earthed'. A qualified electrician or someone like the National Grid should be able to do this for you.

A modern consumer unit will look something like this:

Many people do not think about looking at the number of plug sockets per room. Normally, you will want at least two double sockets per room for a regular buy-to-let and at least three double sockets per room for an HMO (House of Multiple Occupation). For commercial properties, such as offices, then you will probably want more sockets per room.

Just keep an eye out for the amount of plug sockets the next time that you are looking around a property. The less plug sockets per room normally means that the costs of electrical installation will be higher.

3. Roof Tiles/Chimney Stack

The roof is a very important aspect of a property. If there are tiles missing or the pointing is bad, then this could allow water into the property through the roof which could lead to significant issues further on down the line.

Many people fail to even look at the roof when viewing property and this is very worrying. The roof is one of the key aspects to look at because it can be one of the most expensive parts of the house to replace or repair.

The chimney isn't something that people would necessarily consider looking at. However, it is important to do so. Just make sure that it is in good condition, the brickwork is tidy, the stack isn't leaning or wonky in any way, that it is capped off if necessary and that the flashing surrounding it is in good order.

The easiest way to look at the roof and chimney stack is to get a pair of binoculars and to have a look through them. Be careful where you use binoculars though as people might start to think that you are trying to peep through their windows!

I've never had this happen to me before, but you do hear of some really odd stories out there in the property world.

If you do decide to get a survey done on the property (always recommended), then the surveyor will have a good look at the roof as well. They may use a ladder to gain access to the roof, but that is up to them.

4. Guttering

Examine the guttering at the front and rear of the property. Is it wooden? Is the main down pipe (the giant pipe that is attached vertically to the roof) uPVC or cast iron? Is the guttering leaking?

Many simple issues in property can be resolved by the guttering. The great thing about guttering is that it is relatively simple to replace and it doesn't cost too much.

If the guttering is blocked, old, wooden or leaking, then this could lead to water ingress through the roof or potentially lead to damp patches in the property itself.

Ideally, you will want new uPVC guttering with a uPVC down pipe. Fitted properly, you will find that this will help to keep your investment property from suffering from water ingress and damp on the upper levels.

5 Damp

There are two forms of damp: i) normal damp (which can happen as a result of water ingress as explained in the Guttering section), or, ii) rising damp, which rises from the ground and affects the lower parts of the property.

Rising damp usually rises to a level of around one metre from the base of the floor and the remedies are either to hack off the plaster, skim and re-plaster the walls or to hack off the plaster and to apply a damp proof course (DPC). This costs a lot more money but is worth it, especially as you can get warrantees on DPC's.

Rising damp looks like this: (picture sourced from http://www.dampandtimberguard.com/rising-damp/)

You can pick up a damp proof meter from places such as Screwfix or B&Q and this tool is really useful. You can put it up against a wall and it will tell you if the wall is damp or not. Genius!

Nine times out of ten, damp is very easy to spot. The walls will be wet, the walls will be discoloured, and the affected rooms will smell very musty.

Normal damp can occur when the brickwork has been wet for a long time or over a sustained period of time when there has been no air circulating in the property.

Always check the guttering and roof as water ingress there can lead to patches of damp due to excessive water hitting the walls.

Two other key areas of note:

Kitchens and bathrooms are the two main areas that will add significant value to your investment property. Look at them carefully and judge whether or not they need upgrading. If they are already suitable for the area, then they do not necessarily need replacing/upgrading.

If they are in a poor condition, then it is advisable to upgrade them as this will add value.

Summary

There are many different things to look out for when you are viewing properties. The five things in this article are designed to help you to keep your eyes peeled for both common and not-so-common things (such as plug sockets). Make a note and then look out for them when you are viewing your next property.

Ways To Price The Cost Of Potential Works

How Do I Know How Much It Will Cost?

This is a great question. You can find out in one of two ways. One way would be to spend hours and hours researching all the potential items online at trade price and then you will have a very good idea of the purchase price of the products.

The second way would be to go around the investment property with a builder and see what they say. A good, local and recommended builder will be able to tell you roughly how much things will cost.

If you are still unsure at this stage then you could get a rough itemised estimate from the builder and then do some internet research to see if the numbers are roughly the same.

It is always good to have some knowledge of rough refurbishment costs and to know what you want from your refurbishment. Being indecisive isn't advantageous as builders (not necessarily all of them) may sense this and add £50 here and £50 there for things that aren't essential.

As previously mentioned, a builder is an essential part of your power team and they will have the experience necessary in order to price the works.

It is always advantageous to get at least three quotes before deciding which builder you would like to work with.

If you do not have any builders, then ask fellow investors in the area. Ask local estate and lettings agents or even if you are driving around the streets and see some works going on, then pop in and speak to the builder directly.

All builders are going to have their own relationships with suppliers, their own costs and their own ways of doing things.

Your builder could also project manage the refurbishment as well. This is especially useful if you are based in one part of the country and the builder/property in another.

There really is no general rule of thumb when it comes to the cost of a refurb, as prices will depend on a number of factors:

- Where in the country your property is (eg. London is more expensive than Hull for a similar refurb).

- What specification/finish is being put onto the works.

- Your tenant target market.

- The builder.

- Your exit strategy.

These five factors will play a big role in determining the price of the refurb.

This book is about How To Buy Your First Buy-to-Let, so it is assumed that your exit strategy is to let the property. However, do bear in mind that if you do decide to buy and sell property, then this exit strategy normally involves a higher-quality finish on your refurb, thus increasing the costs.

Refurbishment Bonus Tip!

LNPG

The Landlords' National Property Group (LNPG) has fantastic access to retailers, furniture companies, solicitors, kitchen suppliers, bathroom suppliers and so much more. LNPG can help you to save a lot of money during the refurbishment process and on all other aspects of property too.

If this is something that you would like to explore, then e-mail rob@thepropertynomads.com and I will pass over your contact details to LNPG. They will then ring you to explain more about their fantastic services.

Plenty of landlords use them and they are highly recommended.

Five Top Ways To Analyse Buy-To-Lets

Analysing a deal can be complicated. Over time, we have found that there are five main ways to effectively analyse a property deal, specifically buy-to-lets.

There are so many different measurables involved that effectively analysing a deal can seem to be quite a long and drawn out process. Trust me, it does not have to be.

Now, I don't know how many times you have picked up the phone to an estate or lettings or even a sourcing agent to be told, "the yield on this property is a fantastic 8.2%" or something along those lines.

If you are like me, you don't really care for gross yield but instead either the cashflow or net yield, or even the net return on investment after refinance. You will have your own preferred way to analyse your buy-to-lets.

1. Gross Yield

Gross yield = annual rent/purchase price

Therefore, if you get presented with a property where the gross annual rent is £7,200 and the purchase price is £72,000 then your gross yield is 10%.

Gross yield is what a lot of estate agents will use to try and lure you into buying a property.

As an investor though, you are probably wondering what the cashflow is?

This is the challenge with gross yield. Until you dive deep into the numbers, you will not be able to know.

Gross yield doesn't take into account mortgage payments, void periods, MOE (Monthly Operating Expenses) or even management fees.

Gross yield can be used as a very basic indicator for an analysis.

There are investors that solely base their investment decisions on gross yield. There is nothing wrong with this and if that is what works for them, then superb.

As we always say, as long as everything you do is under the ethical win-win umbrella, and it works for you, then there is no right or wrong in property.

2. Net Yield

Net yield gives you a much better understanding as it takes into account management fees, MOE and mortgage payments.

To calculate net yield, you need to deduct all the expenses from the gross annual rental income. You then divide that number by the purchase price of the property and multiply by 100.

Example

Net Yield = (gross annual income) - costs per annum/property value x 100

If you had a property that had a gross annual rent of £7,200 with total annual costs of £3,600, then your net yield would be 5%. This is a big difference from the gross yield of 10% on a property with exactly the same rent and purchase price.

It is more than likely that your net yield figure will always be lower than your gross yield figure as net yield is designed to take into account the costs associated with running a property.

3. Net Return on Cash Left in Deal

Net return on cash left in deal (or Net ROI) is slightly different from net yield as Net ROI only takes into account the money that you put into the deal. It does not take into account the amount on the mortgage (if you are purchasing with a mortgage).

Deal Address:	25 Example Street, Hull		B2L	
Purchase Price:	£72,000		Monthly Rent:	£600
Works Budget:	£0		Annual Gross Rent:	£7,200
Source Fee:	£0		Management:	£720
Your Legal Fees:	£1,300		MOE:	£720
Finance & Survey Costs:	£500			

Deal Address:	25 Example Street, Hull		B2L	
Stamp Duty Land Tax	£2,160			
Refinance Costs + Legals	£0			
Total Investment	£75,960		Annual Net Rent:	£5,760
Total Investment with Deposit	£21,960		Monthly Net Rent:	£480
Mortgage LTV:	75%			
Mortgage Amount:	£54,000		Interest Rate:	3.50%
Deposit Amount	£18,000		Annual Mortgage Cost:	£1890.00
			Monthly Mortgage Cost:	£157.50
			Monthly Cashflow:	£322.50
			Yearly Cashflow:	£3870.00
Gross Yield		10.00%		
NET ROI on Cash Left In Deal:		17.62%		

The above example shows that the legal fees, finance and survey costs and Stamp Duty Land Tax (SDLT) are taken into consideration.

Also, you will see from the column on the left that there is a total investment of £75,960 (if no mortgage is needed) or a total of £21,960 assuming that a 75% LTV mortgage is taken out and that the bank will lend you £54,000 (as long as you pay the 25% deposit which equates to £18,000).

Note how the Net ROI jumps up to 17.62% when a mortgage is taken out.

Also, note the cashflow of £322.50. Cashflow is incredibly important in property and some investors will only invest in a property if they know that the cashflow is above a particular amount per month.

Net ROI provides a more in-depth analysis than gross or net yield and is also able to provide you with a likely monthly and annual cashflow figure for a property. This is the most important dynamic for some investors.

4. Net Return on Cash Left in Deal After Refinance

Net return on cash left in deal after refinance is the other metric that you can use to effectively analyse a buy-to-let or HMO.

This metric only works if you know that you are getting a discount on the original purchase price.

If you are not getting a discount on the original purchase price or the property has not been undervalued in any way, then Net ROI after refinance will probably not be applicable.

After Refinance				
			Monthly Rent:	£600
			Annual Gross Rent:	£7,200
			Management:	£720
			MOE:	£720
			Annual Net Rent:	£5,760
			Monthly Net Rent:	£480
End Valuation:	£90,000			
Refinance LTV:	75%		Interest Rate:	3.50%
Maximum Refinance:	£67,500		Annual Mortgage Cost:	£2,362.50
			Monthly Mortgage Cost:	£196.88
Cash Left In Deal:	£8,460			
			Monthly Cashflow:	£283.13
			Yearly Cashflow:	£3,397.50
NET ROI on Cash In Deal After Refinance:	40.16%			

For example, if you know that when you buy the £72,000 property that has an annual gross rent of £7,200, that you have bought at a discount and that the true value of the property is £90,000, then you will more than likely want to refinance and get some of your original deposit money back out in the future.

From the table above, you will see that if you refinance onto the same mortgage product (75% LTV at 3.5% interest only per annum) but at a new property value of £90,000 then you will only have £8,460 left in the property deal, with a slightly reduced monthly cashflow of £283.13 yet a Net ROI of 40.16%.

40.16% is much better than the 17.72% Net ROI before refinance and indeed the 5% net yield.

This metric really shows you the true Net ROI of a property should you be able to buy the property at a discount in the first place.

5. Cashflow

It is common for investors to not think about yield too much and to just focus on the cashflow instead. This is perfectly understandable as cashflow is very important in property.

The easiest way to find out what the cashflow of a property is, is to use a calculator like the one that we have. Our cashflow calculator is easy to use and it is able to provide you with a monthly cashflow figure. It was created out of necessity as I couldn't find any decent property cashflow calculators out there.

In order to get your free copy, then head over to www.thepropertynomads.com and subscribe to our newsletter. You'll then be sent your own cashflow calculator for buy-to-let properties straight away!

Other Important Points

You do not have to include MOE when analysing your buy-to-let investments. MOE is something that we (my business partner and I) like to include in our own analysis as we always like to have a cash buffer per property so that in the event of a void period or a refurbishment, we are not panicking about where the money will come from as it will be in the reserve account.

If you are managing your own portfolio, then you do not have to include the cost of management fees when analysing your buy-to-let investments.

However, you should include a management fee because it is a very tax efficient to do so. I'm not FCA regulated or an independent financial adviser (IFA), so you should go and get the necessary and recommended advice about setting up a lettings/management company.

There are always variables. For example, you may decide to have an 80% LTV mortgage or your management fees may be 12.5% rather than 10%. You may decide to have your MOE set at 15% and not 10%. The mortgage interest rate may even be different; it may be higher or indeed lower. The Stamp Duty will inevitably be different too, along with the costs of legals and the finance.

The simple Buy-to-Let Deal Analyser is designed to allow that flexibility so that you can tailor to your property needs and numbers.

Summary

There are five main ways to effectively analyse a buy-to-let property. Each method is slightly different and you have to do what works for you. There is no right or wrong as your property business is yours and your metrics are yours.

It is highly recommended though that you base your investments on cash flow.

Knowing Your Numbers

Before you put any offers in with agents it is important to stress a couple of things.

Firstly, you will hear a lot of people talk about Money In, Money Out (MIMO) or No Money Left In (NMLI) deals and recycling your deposit so that you can take all of it back out and then re-invest it into your next property.

This is certainly achievable in buy-to-lets but please do not get so hung up on doing so.

Sometimes deposit monies are left in the deal and this is not the end of the world.

I'll show you what I mean.

Let's say that you've followed all the steps and that you have found some great properties online that are in your goldmine area and that you know that properties are worth £100,000 when sold.

You have viewed a couple of properties in that area that need £10,000 worth of refurbishment work doing to them.

These properties are currently on the market for £90,000.

The buying numbers with a mortgage will look like this.

Deal Address:	Example Street		B2L	
Purchase Price:	£90,000		Monthly Rent:	£650
Works Budget:	£10,000		Annual Gross Rent:	£7,800
Source Fee:	£0		Management:	£780
Legal Fees:	£1,200		MOE:	£780
Finance & Survey Costs:	£500			
Stamp Duty Land Tax	£2,700			
Refinance Costs + Legals	£0			

Deal Address:	Example Street		B2L	
Total Investment	£104,400		Annual Net Rent:	£6,240
Total Investment with Deposit	£36,900		Monthly Net Rent:	£520
Mortgage LTV:	75%			
Mortgage Amount:	£67,500		Interest Rate:	5.00%
Deposit Amount	£22,500		Annual Mortgage Cost:	£3,375.00
			Monthly Mortgage Cost:	£281.25
			Monthly Cashflow:	£238.75
			Yearly Cashflow:	£2,865.00
Gross Yield		8.67%		
NET ROI on Cash Left In Deal:		7.76%		

You will see from these numbers that the total deposit (including the mortgage, stamp duty, cost of the refurbishment works, legal fees and broker/finance fees) is £36,900.

That's ok. However, if the DUV (Done Up Value) of the property is only £100,000, then when you go to refinance then your numbers will look like this.

After Refinance				
			Monthly Rent:	£650
			Annual Gross Rent:	£7,800
			Management:	£780
			MOE:	£780
			Annual Net Rent:	£6,240
			Monthly Net Rent:	£520
End Valuation:	£100,000			
Refinance LTV:	75%		Interest Rate:	5.00%
Maximum Refinance:	£75,000		Annual Mortgage Cost:	£3,750.00

After Refinance				
			Monthly Mortgage Cost:	£312.50
Cash Left In Deal:	£29,400			
			Monthly Cashflow:	£207.50
			Yearly Cashflow:	£2,490.00
NET ROI on Cash In Deal After Refinance:	8.47%			

You can see that there is way too much money left in this deal. Way too much! In an ideal world, you do not want any money left in a deal. There is a caveat with this that I will touch upon in a bit.

Let's say that we need all of our money out of this deal. So what should we offer? By playing around on the calculator, we can see that £61,500 is the best that you can offer.

Deal Address:	Example Street		B2L	
Purchase Price:	£61,500		Monthly Rent:	£650
Works Budget:	£10,000		Annual Gross Rent:	£7,800
Source Fee:	£0		Management:	£780
Legal Fees:	£1,200		MOE:	£780
Finance & Survey Costs:	£500			
Stamp Duty Land Tax	£1,845			
Refinance Costs + Legals	£0			
Total Investment	£75,045		Annual Net Rent:	£6,240
Total Investment with Deposit	£28,920		Monthly Net Rent:	£520
Mortgage LTV:	75%			
Mortgage Amount:	£46,125		Interest Rate:	5.00%
Deposit Amount	£15,375		Annual Mortgage Cost:	£2,306.25
			Monthly Mortgage Cost:	£192.19
			Monthly Cashflow:	£327.81

Deal Address:	Example Street		B2L	
			Yearly Cashflow:	£3,933.75
Gross Yield		12.68%		
NET ROI on Cash Left In Deal:		13.60%		

You will see that the total investment required for this purchase is now £28,920.

After Refinance				
			Monthly Rent:	£650
			Annual Gross Rent:	£7,800
			Management:	£780
			MOE:	£780
			Annual Net Rent:	£6,240
			Monthly Net Rent:	£520
End Valuation:	£100,000			
Refinance LTV:	75%		Interest Rate:	5.00%
Maximum Refinance:	£75,000		Annual Mortgage Cost:	£3,750.00
			Monthly Mortgage Cost:	£312.50
Cash Left In Deal:	£45			
			Monthly Cashflow:	£207.50
			Yearly Cashflow:	£2,490.00
NET ROI on Cash In Deal After Refinance:		5533.33%		

A Net ROI of 5533.33%. That's pretty cool, eh? And a cashflow of £207.50 per month.

Assuming that the property does revalue at £100,000, then you will get back £28,885 of your original £28,920 investment, only leaving £45 in your investment.

Do you ALWAYS have to get ALL of your money back out?

No, is the short answer.

I have a few properties that have around £10,000 left in each of them after refinance. That is not bad in my opinion. Let me show you an example of a property that is currently in the portfolio.

Deal Address:	Example Street		B2L	
Purchase Price:	£40,000		Monthly Rent:	£400
Works Budget:	£8,800		Annual Gross Rent:	£4,800
Source Fee:	£0		Management:	£480
Legal Fees:	£1,200		MOE:	£480
Finance & Survey Costs:	£500			
Stamp Duty Land Tax	£0			
Refinance Costs + Legals	£0			
Total Investment	£50,500		Annual Net Rent:	£3,840
Total Investment with Deposit	£20,500		Monthly Net Rent:	£320
Mortgage LTV:	75%			
Mortgage Amount:	£30,000		Interest Rate:	5.00%
Deposit Amount	£10,000		Annual Mortgage Cost:	£1,500.00
			Monthly Mortgage Cost:	£125.00
			Monthly Cashflow:	£195.00
			Yearly Cashflow:	£2,340.00
Gross Yield	12.00%			
NET ROI on Cash Left In Deal:	11.41%			

After Refinance					
			Monthly Rent:		£400
			Annual Gross Rent:		£4,800
			Management:		£480
			MOE:		£480
			Annual Net Rent:		£3,840
			Monthly Net Rent:		£320
End Valuation:	£58,000				
Refinance LTV:	75%		Interest Rate:		5.00%
Maximum Refinance:	£43,500		Annual Mortgage Cost:		£2,175.00
			Monthly Mortgage Cost:		£181.25
Cash Left In Deal:	£7,000				
			Monthly Cashflow:		£138.75
			Yearly Cashflow:		£1,665.00
NET ROI on Cash In Deal After Refinance:		23.79%			

As long as our NET ROI after refinance is over 20%, then we will buy that property. This is just a personal metric. You may decide that you want a higher or lower NET ROI after refinance. The Holy Grail is to get an infinite NET ROI and that is definitely achievable.

However, the caveat is that you can seriously piss off the estate agents with continual cheeky offers.

If we go back to the first example of the property that is on the market for £90,000: if you know that the DUV is £100,000 and that £10,000 of works need doing to it, then will the agent or the vendor really accept £61,500?

The answer is that you will only ever know by putting the offer in. You do not know the vendor's circumstances or their reason for selling. Only the vendor and the estate agent will know that. No harm in asking though!

Through my years in property investing, it is fair to say that there is a fine line between working with the estate agents and severely pissing them off and ruining relationships with continual low-ball offers.

On a personal note, I'd rather not continually dance the dance with estate agents, so am always happy to pay a good, reliable sourcing agent a fee for securing properties below market value (BMV).

You do not necessarily have to use your own money to buy property either. Read the Joint Ventures (JV) section to find out how to team up with others and how to raise finance.

Joint Ventures

There are many different ways in which to raise finance.

If you do not have your own savings or finances, then you will have to either joint venture (JV) or use other people's money (OPM). It is entirely plausible to use other people's monies in order to pay for your property investments.

This section will look at joint venture partnerships and ways in which you could raise finance.

What is a Joint Venture Partnership?

There is a subtle difference between an investor and a joint venture partner.

A joint venture partner is likely to be more hands-on than an investor and will normally take a much larger interest in the property and the deal.

The standard definition of a joint venture partnership is "when two or more persons come together to form a temporary partnership for the purpose of carrying out a particular project."

Doing a joint venture (JV) can be very easy or it can be very difficult. It really depends on how easy or difficult you want to make it and how easy or difficult your JV partner wants to make it.

You have probably heard lots of stories of successful JV partnerships and also partnerships that have not been so successful.

What Makes A Good JV?

A good JV is when people come together for the greater good and are able to focus on producing the results. The key thing in a JV is that everyone is a winner and there should not be any losers.

How Do You Set Up A JV?

It is important to remember that JVs and property in general are both people businesses. Sometimes that means that it takes time to build these relationships through networking and talking to people. Numerous coffees will more than likely be consumed during this process.

Setting up a JV is quite straightforward. The easy way to do it is to keep talking and keep communicating with each party involved in the JV and produce a heads of terms document.

A heads of terms document starts out as a blank piece of paper.

The heads of terms document will include information such as who wants what in the JV, what the purpose and the desired outcome of the JV is, and what the roles and responsibilities are of everyone involved in project.

Personal details and company information will be on the heads of terms document too.

Other key factors that you will need to put into the heads of terms will include what happens if the project goes wrong. Obviously you hope (and we certainly hope) that the project is not going to go wrong.

You do, however, hear stories of projects that have gone wrong and where the people within the JV have fallen out with each other as there is no clear Plan A, Plan B or even any form of exit strategy.

The last thing you would want (or indeed your JV partner would want), is for something to go wrong and for them to be without any form of contingency plan or understanding as to how to sort it out.

While these cases are fairly few and far between, it is important that you know your exit strategies for the project and also who is going to do what in the event of something going wrong.

Finally, once you have as much information as possible on your heads of terms, then you will need to take it to your solicitor who will write it up with all of the extra legal words and phrases to complement what you have done and you will have a JV agreement as a result.

Structure Of A Joint Venture

There are many different types of company structure that can be used for a joint venture. Each has their own tax advantages and some structures may be more beneficial to you than others.

It is highly recommended that you seek the relevant professional advice before deciding on your exact structure. Speak to a qualified individual such as a tax planner as they will be able to help you.

Common JVs

It is quite common to have a JV that is 50/50 which involves:

- Having one person (or more) putting in the *time and skills* and other person putting in the money.
- Having one person (or more) putting in the *time* and other person putting in the money.
- Two or more people putting in *equal amounts of time and money* into a deal.

You can JV on anything as long as everyone is happy and understands their roles and responsibilities. You may JV on buy-to-lets, HMOs, land development, commercial conversions, serviced accommodation and any other property strategies that you can think of.

The Secret C – Communication

Communication is fundamental to the success of a JV.

Property is all about people, building trust and working with others. It is important to be able to master the art of communication and to be able to communicate effectively.

Set out your communication channels from the start. How will you communicate? Phone? Email?

It is possible that there will be times in your JV where you must share some bad news or some news that may affect the outcome of the project. This will need to be communicated to the other parties no matter how bad it may be.

Do not fear sharing the bad news as it is life, it is property and these things are here to test us.

Communication is very important in these situations as trying to shy away from bad news will more than likely have a negative impact on everyone involved.

Nine times out of ten anything can be worked out with a quick chat, coffee and an open and honest conversation. There is nothing to be fearful of in these situations, as in a JV you are a team and most teams will end up working together for the greater good.

Key Tip – Communicate via different channels such as email, WhatsApp or even Facebook Messenger.

THE SECRET T – TIME

Setting up a JV can take time.

This is because it can take time to build up the relationships prior to entering into a JV.

You do hear stories of people who have just met and then decide to go into business and become incredibly successful very quickly. Fair play to them!

However, these stories are few and far between and time will more than likely be required in order to find the right people to work with.

Building relationships is important in general and it is the same when it comes to JVs. You wouldn't necessarily jump into bed with the first person that you see on a night out, so you don't have to jump into bed with the first person that you see when it comes to doing a JV in property.

Good things come to those that wait.

Building rapport with others does not happen overnight and it does take time. Just because someone has a complementary skill-set or money, it does not mean that you will end up working very well together. This is why regular meetings are important and why building the rapport is essential.

Six Key Questions To Consider When Looking For A JV Partner

There are six important questions that you should be asking yourself when looking for a potential JV partner.

1. Do they have what you want?
2. Do they have what you need?
3. Do you get on well with them?
4. Do you have what they want?
5. Do you have what they need?
6. Do they get on well with you?

It is important to remember that although you will be looking for a JV partner, they may also be looking for one as well. Therefore, they will be asking the same questions.

A JV is not all about you, you, you, nor is it all about them, them, them. It is about providing each other with complementary skill-sets and complementary qualities that go hand in hand.

Knowing what each person wants and needs is crucial in forming the basis of a JV.

Summary

Although there are some very common JV set-ups out there, in reality there is no set way for how a JV should work.

Every JV starts with a blank piece of paper in which you will write down heads of terms. Every JV is likely to be different because of the people involved, what people are putting in and what people want out of the project.

There is no right or wrong when it comes to a JV with others as everything will be on the heads of terms and will be cleared to all parties during the legal process.

A JV is all about creating win-win situations and working with people.

Doing a JV is no different to anything else that involves working with people. This is because you are essentially relying on people communicating with others and working with people in order to achieve a common goal.

Where To Find JV Partners

Money is pretty much everywhere. The secret is to find the places that give you the best chance of being with people that are likely to have it.

Property Networking Events

Property Networking Events are very useful. Progressive Property Network events (PPN), Property Investor Networking (PIN) and Property Hub meetups are all superb examples of property-related networking events.

People turn up to property events for numerous reasons. They may want to find out more about property, they may already be investing in property or they may have money but are not sure what to do with it. Equally, people such as interior designers will attend as they have superb opportunities in which to grow their own businesses and network.

The key is to get around the room and introduce yourself to as many people as possible and build that rapport through conversations. Always follow up too because you never know who you are going to meet and what is going to happen. Just get out and about and speak to people to build your network.

Local Business Networking Events

Business Networking International (BNI) is a very good example of a local event. BNI meetings are in many places and consist of local business people coming together to network, share and pass on business to each other. There is normally room for a property investor and/or developer.

Your investment area or the area where you live is likely to have a local chamber of commerce. They are relatively inexpensive to join and can provide some superb opportunities. Local business people get together regularly in order to discuss what is going on in the local area. Not many people will have a knowledge in property and you will be able to position yourself as an expert. This could create opportunities over time too.

Social Media

Social media is a fantastic place to raise finance. People watch each other on the various platforms such as Facebook, Twitter, Instagram and LinkedIn. You never know who will be watching your projects, deals or your property journey.

Keep showing people what you are doing, keep adding value to other people, and be consistent. I myself have raised £15,000 through Facebook, just by posting about various projects that were being undertaken, various BMV opportunities in my local area, local investment news, photos and information too. There are people out there that have raised a lot more through social media.

High-End Clubs And Restaurants

It is common to hear stories about attending selective clubs (high-end gentlemen's clubs in London, for example), talking to club members and then being offered a lot of money. The fact of the matter is that people with money will spend time in establishments that are of a high standard.

It is unlikely that you will ever overhear a conversation in a McDonald's about a multi-million pound development, whereas you may hear that conversation in a high-end restaurant or at a high-end club.

Sports Clubs And Gyms

Do you play golf? Do you know of a Rotary Club near you?

It is always beneficial to mix passion and profession. If you already play golf, enjoy shooting, going to the gym or helping others (Rotary Clubs), then you are already in a great position.

A lot of people that undertake these activities do so for various reasons: they enjoy it and, more importantly, they have the time to do it.

If people have time to do what they love to do, then chances are that they are either retired, have money or both.

Attend and get talking to people. Build rapport and tell people what you do. If you do not tell people what you do, then they will never know.

Six Ninja Hints To Find Investors/Joint Venture Partners

Ninja Hint #1

Network with a purpose. Know what you are going networking for and set yourself goals. If you know that the end goal is to raise x amount of pounds, then your objective for every networking event may be to meet three new people and get their business cards and follow up.

It is better to have a target such as this rather than just turning up without a focus.

If time is precious to you, then make the most out of your networking by having focus and by knowing what you are going for.

Ninja Hint #2

Always follow up if you take someone else's business card. It is crucial to follow up on the next day or two. It is one thing to make great connections, yet the rapport and relationship has to be worked on. Therefore, always follow up with a "hello" and a "thank you for your time" email or call. This will keep the rapport building going.

Ninja Hint #3

Do not just rely on one form of networking event to start. Try and attend as many different types of networking events as possible. Use a blend to start off with. You will find over time that some networking events will be more beneficial than others. When you have what you want, then do not necessarily quit networking. In fact, you should never quit networking, but instead pick and choose what works for you.

Ninja Hint #4

Tell people what you do and (ideally) where you do it.

When you are at a networking event or at a rotary club, rather than saying, "I'm a property investor" try saying something along the lines of, "I help people make money in property", "I find properties for investors in Hull" or "I provide property solutions for people who are in need of help."

A property investor could mean many different things. In order to stand out from the crowd when talking to others, try to be creative with your opening line. Telling someone that you help people make money in property is more likely to provoke a response and start a conversation than just saying you are a property investor.

Ninja Hint #5

Add value to other people. The law of reciprocity says that: when someone does something nice for you, you will have a deep-rooted psychological urge to do something nice in return. That is just the tip of the iceberg as it is quite common for people to reciprocate with a gesture far more generous than the original good deed.

So if you are adding value to others by sharing your story, sharing your challenges and information about something and by offering to help others, then you may find that those same people that you have helped will in turn help you further on down the line.

Ninja Hint #6

If you have an investment opportunity then tell people about it. Meet up with people and share the details.

Carry a brochure or investment document around with you at all times. Share it with people and do not ask, "Do you have the money for this?" Instead say, "If you know of anyone that would be interested, then please get them to get in touch with me." This is a very subtle way of asking.

The same applies to social media. If the deal is secure it is best to give out some numbers and what you are looking for, with a call to action such as "e-mail me at ... or call me on... for further information."

SUMMARY

Money is everywhere. Your network is your net worth, so be with people who are going to add value to your life and your business. Network, attend events, think where people with money normally spend their time and go and spend your time there too. Add value to others, build rapport over time and this will help to build crucial relationships and trust.

If you have a deal or a project, then show it to people and ask if they know of anyone that would be interested. You never know, they may have the money sitting in the bank ready and waiting. If you do strike it lucky very quickly with a contact with money, then that is superb and many congratulations!

Putting Offers In With Agents

You have viewed properties, you have done your area analysis, you know what the properties are worth. Now you put your offers in to the agents.

There are two alternative scripts that you can use when you are "not making an offer".

They may go something like this:

"I'm not going to make an offer (give reason), (pause). But if I was, it would be…"

"I don't want to make a low offer, but if I was to offer it might be (vague offer) and (give reason)."

These two things are great as you will not come across as being offensive with your offers and you will have explanations as to why your offers are what they are.

You are also sowing the seeds into the head of the estate agent.

Always give a reason as this will help to boost credibility with the agents. You will not want to be perceived as a time waster.

Property negotiation is all a game of cat and mouse at the end of the day.

It is possible that you will get a LOT of rejections before you get an offer accepted. Do not worry about that. It is possible that your first offer gets accepted! You never know unless you are out there putting your offers in.

Put offers in on all the properties that you view.

If necessary, then put these offers in writing as well as you will be able to explain in depth why you have offered what you have and have a paper trail too.

If you view a lot of property and then do not put offers in, then the agents may perceive you as a time waster. This is not a perception that you want.

Consistency and longevity are phenomenal in property.

Keep a spreadsheet of all of the properties that you have viewed and offered on and remember to follow up every four weeks or so. Sometimes a property may be "sold" but quite a high proportion of property sales fall through, so there is always fortune in the follow up.

Just keep going, be consistent, be persistent and you WILL get an offer accepted eventually.

Proof Of Funds

Both the estate agent and your solicitor will require proof of funds. Your solicitor will want and need to know where that money has come from as they will need to adhere to anti-money laundering policies.

The estate agent will want to see proof of funds, just so they know that you are not wasting their time.

It is best practice to have an electronic copy of proof of funds (with your bank details edited out) as you will be able to e-mail this to both the agent and your solicitor. A proof of funds will look something like this:

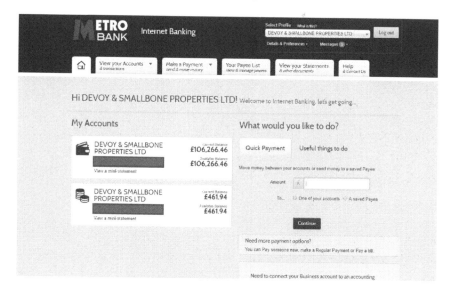

Or something like this:

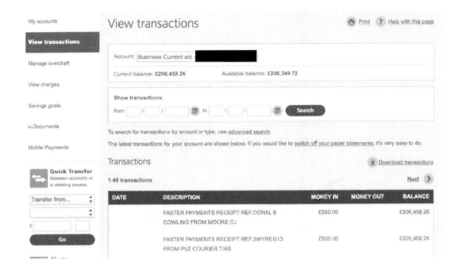

Don't forget to edit your bank details so that no account information is shown. I forgot to do that once and my business partner was not very impressed to say the least!

Relocating vs. Travelling To And From Your Investment Area

Having attended many property events and listened to many new property investors that are keen to get started in their property investing journeys, this is one of the most common dilemmas that comes up and people sometimes take way too long to think of their solution.

From experience, if you have the circumstances where you have the ability to move to your investment area then I would suggest that you move. If you are truly dedicated to building your portfolio and really getting to know your area, then it is a no brainer.

If you are like I was at the time when I moved from Reading to Hull in my late twenties – single, no family commitments and with an open traveller's mindset – then you should take advantage of this and just move and submerge yourself in your investment area.

If you are truly dedicated to building your portfolio but do not want to know your area, then you should not move. If you have the money and just want other people to do the work for you whilst you manage from afar, then you should not move.

If your current circumstances do not allow you to move – for example, you have a well-paid job in London where relocation would mean a huge pay cut, moving your children's schools, or something along those lines – then maybe you should not move.

At the end of the day, there is no right or wrong and the decision is entirely down to you.

Re-locating or travelling to and from your investment area really comes down to the time vs. money dilemma.

Time vs. Money – The Ultimate Dilemma

There are four key questions to ask yourself.

1. How much time do you have?
2. How much money do you have?
3. What sacrifices are you prepared to make in the short term in order to benefit in the long term?
4. How far are you prepared to travel?

Let's look at these three questions individually.

1. How much time do you have?

Think about your situation.

*   Do you have kids?
*   Do you have a needy spouse?
*   How much time does your work take per week?
*   How long is your commute?
*   Where do you live?

If you have a lot of time on your hands, then the chances are you will be happy to drive up and down the country looking for properties, investigating different areas, offering on properties and building your business.

If you have a really high-octane job, work 60 to 70 hours a week, only get Sunday off and then you have to spend time with your spouse, then chances are that you will not want to spend that time travelling up and down the country investigating different areas, offering on property and building your business.

Knowing how much time you realistically have available will help you to determine your property strategy.

2. How much money do you have?

This question is important as this (combined with the time) will help you to determine your property strategy.

If you have £3,000,000 sitting in the bank as you read this, then chances are that you may not want to build up a buy-to-let portfolio, but instead focus on commercial conversions.

If you have £25,000 sitting in the bank as you read this, then maybe you are thinking about splitting that down, going to a relatively prosperous yet inexpensive part of the country and buying a couple of buy-to-lets.

If you have £3,000,000 sitting in the bank AND you have NO time, then maybe you would want to team up with someone that will be able to find, renovate and then let properties for you? Or possibly joint venture with someone that has a LOT of time.

If you have £25,000 sitting in the bank AND you have NO time, then maybe you would want to team up with someone that will be able to find, renovate and then let properties for you?

Maybe you are sitting there with no money at all, but plenty of time. Do not worry! There are strategies out there for you. You may be able to forge great relationships with local agents and then network and find people who have money. You could always look at property strategies with low-entry fees such as rent-to-rent, lease options or joint venturing.

How much money you have or don't have sitting in the bank will have a bearing on which property strategy you decide to choose.

3. What sacrifices are you prepared to make in the short term in order to benefit in the long term?

This is a great question to ask yourself. We outlined the importance of having a "why" earlier on and this question ties in perfectly to that.

If you really HATE your job and want to sack your boss and want to be able to grow a property portfolio that produces income per month for you, then maybe you will want to go to the ends of the earth to achieve that.

- Maybe you do not have to go to the football every Saturday?
- Maybe you do not have go out with your work colleagues and have drinks every Friday night?
- Maybe you do not have to go on that holiday right now?

Yes! I can hear the groans as you read those last three bullet points!

If you want something badly enough, then you will find a way to achieve it. You will either make your excuses or just do what you need to do.

I don't write these sentences lightly. I'm not forcing you to not go to football or not go out with your friends. The choice is down to you at the end of the day. There is no right or wrong and it all comes down to how much you want it.

4. How far are you prepared to travel?

This is not a common question that is asked but it is a very important one. For the purposes of this example, we will assume that you live in Penzance, Cornwall, and are looking to invest in buy-to-let properties.

If you are prepared to travel seven and a half hours to Newcastle upon Tyne in order to invest in buy-to-lets, then that is absolutely great. You are obviously prepared to travel over 400 miles (one way) to achieve your dreams and goals. It is on journeys like this that you have to have that strong mentality and you have to know your why!

If you were only prepared to travel within Cornwall in order to invest in buy-to-lets, then your task will certainly be more challenging as you may find that not many areas work well for buy-to-lets within Cornwall.

If you were only prepared to travel within Cornwall, but then found out that buy-to-lets are not a great investment as the prices and yields are too low, then you have two options.

1.   Change your strategy to fit in with Cornwall.
2.   Travel further and find a place does work for buy-to-lets (eg, South Wales).

This principle can be applied anywhere in the country. Think about where you live and how far you are prepared to travel in order to get what you want.

Think about this, your time, your resources and your why.

These four questions are crucial as they can help to determine your property strategy.

It is always recommended that you invest in at least a couple of buy-to-lets first as they will give you your training wheels. They will help you to get your head around the processes and people involved in buying a property, renovating a property, letting a property and re-mortgaging a property.

Using A Property Sourcing Agent To Find Properties For You

What Is A Sourcing Agent And What Do They Do?

If time is a factor for you, then you may decide to buy your properties from a property sourcing agent.

If you have done your homework on your goldmine areas, you know what properties you need to have, you know where the demand is and what the rough numbers are, then this will put you in good stead to be able to work with a property sourcing agent.

What is a sourcing agent?

A sourcing agent is effectively someone who will find you a property that meets your property investing requirements. Sourcing agents can find deals through a number of means and methods and their job is to match up properties with the right buying clients – in other words, you.

Why would you want to use a sourcing agent?

This is a great question and a very commonly asked one too. For example, if you invest in Hull and live in Cornwall and you do not want to continually travel to view properties yet you want to build your portfolio, then you may want to consider utilising a person in the area that has relevant sourcing and/or property investment experience.

You may live and invest in Hull, yet you find that you are not able to get great deals or deals as good as other people. In this instance, you may also look to work with a sourcing agent that has better access to deals than you.

You may just not have the time to continually view and offer on property. You may be in a very high octane and time-consuming job and thus need to rely on others to find properties for you. This is where using a sourcing agent will benefit you.

Sourcing agents will charge for finding properties for you and will more than likely charge fees for overseeing the refurbishment from start to finish. If you live in Cornwall (or somewhere not near your investment area) then this comes down to time vs. cost. What is more important to you?

What can a sourcing agent do to get your deal over the line?

This is a great question and it really depends on the type of sourcing agent that you are working with.

Without over-generalising about all sourcing agents, they can normally be put into three different categories:

1) Property Find Only

Some sourcing agents will just find you a property, take a small reservation fee and then take the rest of the monies upon completion of the purchase. You will be left to deal with solicitors and mortgage brokers in order to finance the deal and get the purchase over the line.

2) Property Find + Project Management

Some sourcing agents offer a find and project management service. Their team will be able to manage your project for you and will be able to refurbish the property to whatever standard you are after. Work closely with them so that your property is refurbished to a suitable living standard and to the specific area (i.e. you would not put a £20,000 kitchen into an £80,000 house.)

With such advanced technology nowadays, it is easy to keep up to date with projects via Skype, Zoom, Facebook Messenger and predominantly WhatsApp. Other channels may be available too.

I have a WhatsApp group for each different property and through trial and experience have found that this is what works best for my business partners and I.

You will still be responsible for dealing with the finance and the solicitors in order to push the deal through, and the sourcing agent and their team will be able to take care of the rest.

3) The Full Hands-Off Experience

This is the same as the above with the added bonus of having a local lettings agent (one that the sourcing agent recommends or even the sourcing agent's own lettings agency) manage your property too. As an investor, this can be a completely hands-off experience. This will work for some people but not for others as some people will be happy managing their own property (even from a long distance).

You will still be responsible for dealing with the finance and the solicitors in order to push the deal through and the sourcing agent and their team will be able to take care of the rest.

However, a good and reliable sourcing agent is likely to know very good brokers and solicitors and may even offer a hand-holding process through the deal for you.

What you need to look for in a reliable sourcing agent

A reliable sourcing agent will be a member of a property body, such as The Property Ombudsman (TPO) or the Property Redress Scheme (PRS). This provides extra security for you as in the case of a dispute you can lodge this with the relevant membership body.

A reliable sourcing agent will have Professional Indemnity Insurance. This is essential as it is designed to protect both you and the sourcing agent in the event that something goes wrong. If you are unhappy with a service, then you would be in a position to be able to claim compensation.

A reliable sourcing agent will also be a member of the Information Commissioner's Office (ICO). The ICO make all of the rules and regulations with regards to the use and security of personal data. This ensures that any personal data obtained and used is then stored in a safe and secure way.

A sourcing agent will more than likely need copies of your proof of funds, proof of address, copies of your passport and/or driving licence and possibly your company name and registration number.

As long as the sourcing agent has an ICO registration number, then you will be safer knowing that they have to adhere to certain rules and guidelines about the storage and protection of data.

Working hand in hand with the ICO is the HMRC and anti-money laundering regulations. A sourcing agent must be registered with HMRC with regards to anti-money laundering regulations. This is to protect both the agent and yourself.

It is possible, not always guaranteed, that a sourcing agent will have a website, social media presence or both. If they do, then great as this then gives them an internet presence and allows you to be able to do some due diligence on them. It is not the end of the world if they do not have an internet presence or a social media presence.

Word-of-mouth recommendations can be critical too. If you keep hearing the same name over and over again or a reliable investor has told you about a sourcing agent, then this is a great sign. It's not a guarantee, but it is certainly a step in the right direction if you get told to speak to someone directly as a result of a recommendation.

Do not be afraid to ask a sourcing agent for all of their information as part of your due diligence. Ask them for examples of previous deals and if they have a couple of clients that they can put you in touch with. A good sourcing agent should be happy to do this for you and should have a file of their sourced deals.

Fees can always be a source of contention. A good and reliable sourcing agent will always want to charge a non-refundable reservation fee as this shows that you are serious about buying the property. The reservation fee is normally 50% of the total sourcing fee and should be placed into a client account. The sourcing agent should also have client account insurance in place too.

There should be sufficient paperwork and a clear process about what is paid at what stage and where the monies are to be paid to. Make sure that all the paperwork is clear and that you understand it.

Normally, in the event of the vendor pulling out or there being something adverse in the legal paperwork, you should be able to get your money back. If you decide that you do not want to go ahead with the deal without good reason, then it will be unlikely that you will get your money back. In my personal experience, this is absolutely fair and a reasonable thing to do.

Read the Terms and Conditions of the paperwork beforehand and have a chat with the sourcing agent and explore what would happen in certain situations.

Finally, a credible sourcing agent will undertake due diligence on both yourself and the vendor of the property.

Property is a people business. Take time to build a relationship with your sourcing agent, do your due diligence and, if you are happy with everything, when the time is right or you get presented with a deal, then take action.

A great sourcing agent can be worth their weight in gold.

What To Avoid In A Sourcing Agent

Normally it is all of the above. If the sourcing agent does not come across as being reliable, does not have membership of one of the relevant professional property bodies and your gut instinct tells you not to work with them, then don't.

Try to avoid agents with a dodgy reputation or where other people's personal experiences with them have not been great. Try to avoid a sourcing agent that does not follow the necessary rules and regulations.

What To Do In The Event That Something Goes Wrong

In the event that something goes wrong after you have done your homework on the agent properly, then you really have three options.

Option 1 (the best option) would be to get in contact with the agent, have a chat with them and try to sort it out there and then.

Option 2 would be to make a claim against the sourcing agent using their Professional Indemnity Insurance.

If that does not work and you are still unhappy, then option 3 would be to contact the necessary relevant body (Property Ombudsman or Property Redress Scheme – whatever the sourcing agent is a member of) and put in a complaint against the agent.

In the event that you cannot get in touch with the agent and they are not part of the Property Ombudsman or Redress Scheme, then you really do not have much of a leg to stand on. The only two routes would be to go to a solicitor and take the agent to court or just swallow the pill, learn from the negative experience and do not repeat the mistakes that you have made.

Summary

Property is a people business. Most people want to work with each other and make a fair income at the end of the day. Network with people, get word-of-mouth recommendations, do your homework and build rapport before jumping into bed with people.

There will be good AND bad sourcing agents out there.

Sourcing agents can be a superb part of your power team as they can save you a lot of time and effort and help you to build your property portfolio. Most agents are worth their weight in gold and are an incredibly useful part of your power team.

However, if you do not do your own due diligence properly, and if something does go wrong, then nine times out of ten a simple conversation will normally yield a positive result. If this does not work, then it is up to you to take your complaint to the next level. Just remember to consider: are you at fault in any way and have you learned something?

Further Reading And Thanks

A big thank you to Antoine Malaise for an interview that led to the writing of this section. For further reading on sourcing compliance, it is recommended that you read *Property Sourcing Compliance* by Tina Walsh. Tina was a police officer and now is a sourcing agent, so she is very serious about compliance.

The Property Nomads' Sourcing and Project Management Services

The Property Nomads offer property sourcing and property project management services. In order to discuss your property requirements and how The Property Nomads can help you, contact Matt McSherry at:
matt@thepropertynomads.co.uk

The 20-Step Guide To Buying Your Buy-To-Let Property

You have now got to the stage where you have had an offer accepted and you may have raised some joint venture finance too!

In order to keep things as simple as possible I have devised a 20-step guide that summarises everything for you, making your life easier and something that you will be able to work with step by step. This is how the property buying process should go!

1. Speak to your broker and get a generic decision in principle.

2. Follow the 10-5-2-1 model and pick an area.

3. Speak to three local letting agents and find out where the rental market is strong within your chosen area.

4. Locate a property from Rightmove or another search engine that's in your goldmine area. (Or if a property sourcing agent has bought it to you, then that is fine as well).

5. Contact solicitors to instruct when your offer is accepted. This is important as it's always the first question an estate agent will ask when your offer has been accepted.

6. View the property and make notes for works that need to be done to bring it up to a letting standard and to maximise resale/revaluation figures. Remember that every £1 spent should add £3 value.

7. Make an offer that works within your financial budget or use the "This is not an offer offer" procedure as explained in the Putting Offers In With Agents section.

8. Once you have agreed the price of the purchase, you will need to give the estate agent your solicitor's and broker's details. Make sure that these are ready as it will help you to look more professional.

9. Contact your solicitor and broker with the property address and the estate agent's details (it is always great to put everyone in the same e-mail as this leverages time).

10. Your broker will then proceed to instruct the mortgage application and the surveyor should carry out a survey within the next 7 to 14 days.

11. Once your solicitor has received the contracts from the vendor's solicitors, he/she can start working on searches, enquiries, environmental search and other legal information. Normally your solicitor will ask for search fees or at least a deposit for the fees to be paid at this stage.

12. Once the survey has been carried out, your mortgage offer should be issued within 7 to 21 days to you and your solicitor.

13. You must always go through the valuation report to identify if there are any potential problems with the property and that the mortgage product is correct.

14. If you are happy with everything, you must sign and send it back straight away to the lenders. (Some mortgage companies want to see that you have got independent legal advice and will request that you sign a personal guarantee as well. This is quite common with Limited Company Mortgages nowadays, so do this at this stage too).

15. Once your solicitor has received all information back from the seller's solicitor and he/she is happy then he/she will be in contact to discuss exchange and completion dates.

16. Once you have agreed an exchange and completion date with your solicitor, he/she will send out a completion invoice for you, requesting deposit monies to exchange.

17. Advise your refurb team that you will be collecting the keys to your property.

18. Once your solicitor advises he/she will be exchanging, you MUST insure the property straight away. (Work with your insurance broker to get this done).

19. Once your solicitor has exchanged, then your completion will commonly be seven days later (though exchange and completion can occur on the same day if requested).

20. On the day of completion, the estate agent (if one was involved) will contact you to collect the keys. If not, then your solicitor will contact you instead.

A few things to note:

- Valuations and surveys can sometimes take a lot of time. This will depend on the mortgage company, the schedule of the valuer and your broker as well.

- The length of time to purchase a property can and WILL vary. I have had cash completions done in 28 days, have had a mortgage purchase take two months, four months, and have had to wait three-and-a-half months just to have a survey done on a property.

- Keep chasing your power team every step of the way. Your solicitor and you may have a great connection, but there is no harm in chasing them to make sure that they get their work done; the same with your mortgage broker too.

- Things can go wrong. The valuation might come back a lot lower than expected, the valuer might not be able to gain access to the property, the searches might show something abnormal, or the valuer might just reject the property because of its construction type. Always expect the unexpected in property.

- The above 20 points are a rough guide to how the process *should* work.

- You can get *gazumped* in England and Wales. Just because you have had an offer accepted and have started your legal process, it does not mean that it is legally binding. You could still pull out of the deal, the vendor could still pull out of the deal or, more annoyingly, someone could come in with a higher offer at the last minute and *gazump* you. It is my understanding that you cannot get gazumped in Scotland because once an offer has been accepted then it is binding.

- Enjoy the funny side of property. One of the properties that I bought in 2017 stated that 'gypsies or circuses are not allowed on-site'. That made both my solicitor and I laugh at the time.

Managing the Refurbishment/Renovation

There are five different ways to manage the refurbishment of a property.

1. Do it yourself.
2. Get your builder to manage it.
3. Get your estate agent to manage it.
4. Get your lettings agent to manage it.
5. Get a local project manager/your sourcing agent to manage it.

There is no right or wrong way to manage the refurb of a property.

As mentioned previously, such is the use of Skype, Facebook Messenger and apps such as WhatsApp, it is relatively easy to manage projects from afar nowadays.

A general rule of thumb is that an estate agent/lettings agent or sourcing agent will charge 10% of the refurbishment costs for a project management fee.

Know Your Area/Tenant Profile

You would have done a lot of area research and viewed a lot of houses to know what will work in your area. You will know what prospective tenants like and do not like and what specification the refurb should be done to.

For example, you wouldn't go ahead and put a £10,000 kitchen in a £60,000 house as that would probably not be a sensible thing to do. Yes, the kitchen would look great and I am sure that your tenants would love it, but it would probably not represent a good investment.

If you were buying in an area for capital growth purposes (i.e. South East) and you put a £10,000 kitchen into a £200,000 house, then this would make more sense (but only if the tenant profile was right).

Sometimes it can be easy to get your emotions involved and let them get in the way of business decisions. Property is great fun, hard work and mentally challenging. You have to remember that you are running a business. Don't let your emotions take over, otherwise you will make more mistakes.

If you know your area, your tenant profile and what is working in the market, then stick to that and add a couple of little extra touches (like small canvas paintings and lampshades) in order to make your property stand out in the rental market.

Certifications Your Property MUST Have

In order for your property to be safe and secure, there are certain certifications that you must get at the end of the refurbishment process.

1. A Gas Safety Certificate.
2. An EPC (Energy Performance Certificate).
3. An Electrical Safety Certificate.

Gas Safety Certificate

It is mandatory to have a gas safety certificate for your rental property.

Either ask a Gas Safe registered engineer, or your lettings agent to ask their Gas Safe registered engineer, to provide you with a certificate.

A gas safety certificate is valid for 12 months.

If your property has no gas whatsoever (i.e. a modern electric flat) then no gas safety is needed.

Energy Performance Certificate

An Energy Performance Certificate measures the energy efficiency of your property and is valid for 10 years.

The EPC will also need to have a minimum rating of an E in order for the property to be valid for rental purposes.

There are possible exceptions to the rule. For example, if the property that you are buying is a listed building or if the works to bring the EPC up to an E are ridiculously high in comparison to the cost of the property.

Given the properties that you are likely to buy for buy-to-let purposes, this is unlikely to be an issue for you at all, but is an important thing to remember.

You should be able to find the EPC for your investment property using the online register at https://www.epcregister.com/. If you are unable to find it, then don't worry and get one booked in. Your lettings agent should be able to help you to find the right person.

Electrical Safety Certificate

At the time of writing, it is NOT mandatory for you to have a five-year periodical electrical safety certificate for your buy-to-let properties.

However, in January 2019, The Ministry of Housing, Communities and Local Government (MHCLG) did announce that mandatory electrical testing will be phased in in due course.

My recommendation is that when you are refurbishing your properties you should get your electrics done properly and then certified by having a registered electrical engineer provide you with a valid Electrical Installation Condition Report (EICR).

An Electrical Safety Certificate is something that you can arrange or your lettings agent can arrange.

Two Other Strong Recommendations

1. Ensure that your property has a carbon monoxide detector. You should put a carbon monoxide detector in the same room as the boiler. Sometimes boilers do leak and carbon monoxide is a silent killer. Protect your tenants as best as you can by having one of these in your buy-to-let property.

2. Smoke alarms. Shockingly, you hear stories of landlords or unscrupulous people that do not have smoke alarms in their rental properties. That is abhorrent in my opinion, so please ensure that you put smoke alarms in. You will need at least one on each level in your property: 10-year lithium battery powered smoke alarms work really well. Also, ensure that they are tested every 12 months.

Lettings Agents vs. Self-Managing

Self-managing is not as bad as people make it out to be.

The key questions to think about are:

- Why are you investing?
- What lifestyle do you want?
- Are you an investor or a landlord/landlady?

If you are investing because you are after that lifestyle where you are not dealing constantly with tenants and fixing taps or arranging maintenance, then having a lettings agent to do the work for you is the way forward.

If you would like to experience advertising the property, viewings, tenant referencing, being hands on when dealing with maintenance and management, then feel free to self-manage.

Ask yourself why you are investing in property. Are you investing so you can have more time? If so, then why would you want to self-manage and not pay someone else to take care of the rest?

Try to think about it this way. You may have invested thousands in your property, possibly thousands in the refurbishments, invested in paying a solicitor and a broker, yet are possibly thinking about not investing in a lettings agent at a mere 10 to 15% per month of the total rent? To me, that seems a little bit crazy.

Why would you invest all that money into a property and then not top it off with the investment in an agent who (once you know they do a good job) will pretty much take care of the property and the tenants for you.

If you consider yourself to be an investor, then it is recommended that you invest in having a lettings agent to do the nitty gritty for you.

As they say, you cannot build a house without a solid foundation, so why would you lay all the foundations and then not finish off building the house?

However, if you consider yourself to be a landlord/landlady, then self-managing will most likely be for you. If you have a desire to manage your own properties, then that is your choice and completely up to you.

It simply comes down to the way you think and how you view property.

From experience and knowing what my skills are and are not, my recommendation is that you take your time to research different lettings agents and work with the one that you feel most comfortable with and that does the best job for you. If you do decide that you want to self-manage because you have that skillset, then go ahead and do it. As we have touched upon so many times already in this book, there is no right or wrong way of wanting to manage your portfolio.

Talking of finding your lettings agent...

Six Key Questions To Consider When Searching For Your Lettings Agent

You will also need to let your property out to some tenants so that you can start making money. There are many ways in which this can be done. You can find your own tenants and reference them yourselves or you can use a local lettings agent and get them to do it for you.

There are many questions and things that you will need to think about when trying to find the best lettings agent for you. Always start with personal recommendations! If you know of anyone else that invests in your local area, then it would be prudent to reach out and ask them.

One of our lettings agents has been investing in Hull for over 10 years and we were friends for two years before we decided to use her to let our properties. Relationships take time!

The aim of this section is so that you are able to pick suitable lettings agencies to meet you at your property so that you can receive a rental appraisal from them.

Six key questions that you want to consider when searching for your lettings agent are:

1. Are they local to the area?

If your agent is local to the area then this is a good start as they are likely to have a wealth of local knowledge and will really know the area in which they are operating. This will be key for you.

2. What regulatory bodies do they belong to?

A good lettings agency will be a part of ARLA (Association of Residential Lettings Agency) and one of the following: The Property Redress Scheme or The Property Ombudsman.

If you are buying in Scotland, then your lettings agent has to belong to the National Register of Lettings Agents. You can find out more by visiting https://www.mygov.scot/letting-agent-registration-landlords/

3. Are they a lettings agent only?

This question may strike you as being a bit odd, yet there is a very good reason why you need to know this. The sales side of property generally provides higher income for agencies. If your lettings agent is also a sales agent, then their focus may be on the more profitable side of the business.

As a result, you may be left with junior and apprentice staff dealing with the lettings. This is unlikely to be of great benefit to you.

Would you rather have an agency that is focused on the lettings side? Or a dual agency where your property is there, but will probably receive diluted attention?

4. Do they have a website?

Have a look at their website. We are in the age of the Internet, and most people's instincts will be to look online.

When I moved from Reading to Hull, the first thing I did was to look on Rightmove for a rental property. It is almost like second nature now just to Google something or to go on Rightmove to look at a property.

5. Where do they advertise?

Your lettings agent should belong to at least one or even two of the major property portals, such as Rightmove, Zoopla, OnTheMarket, PrimeLocation or Truffull. The more places that your agent advertises online, then the better this will be for you.

6. Have they rented similar properties to yours recently in regard to location and price?

This will provide you with peace of mind. If your agent has recently rented out similar properties, then this will put you in good stead as this will demonstrate that they have a good grasp of the area.

As with builders and estate agents, it is important to get three of everything so the best suggestion is to book three lettings agents to meet you at your property in order for them to appraise it.

Finding The Right Lettings Agent For You

Picking a suitable lettings agent isn't just about answering those six questions above. This is just the tip of the iceberg.

You will also want to know what procedures your lettings agent has in place.

Once you have three lettings agents lined up to attend your property, you will want to know more about them. Treat this like a job interview. You would want to have the right person for the right role and picking a lettings agent is no different. You want to ensure that you get the crème de la crème.

From experience, there are 15 key service areas that you will need to consider before picking the right lettings agent.

1. Advice and consultation

The agent should be prepared to meet you at your property, at a time convenient to you, to discuss achievable rent and advise on any measures that might be needed to get a good quality tenant quickly.

Beware of agencies that give a too low or too high estimated rental figure. Too low means they are not on top of their game in your area and too high means they are hungry for the business.

Having a rent set too high will more than likely mean that your property will remain empty for longer. After a while, the agent will bring the rent down and only then will it be in line with the other agents.

Does the lettings agent show respect for you and your property? Property is definitely a people business. Does the agent turn up on time? Do they remove shoes on entering the property? Do they emphasise the positive aspects of the property?

What type of tenants do they anticipate renting the property? Professional couples, individuals, families? And what can you do to entice them further?

You would have done some market research to know what type of tenants you need to be aiming for and a good lettings agent will be able to confirm this.

2. Marketing

Marketing your property is fundamental in order to avoid long void periods. Your lettings agent should advertise in a variety of ways:

Online on portals such as Rightmove, Zoopla and OnTheMarket.

Offline i.e. local paper and advertising board at the property itself.

Floorplans are important. Will the lettings agents provide floorplans for your property? If they do, then make sure that you check the price of them as some agents will look to charge a ridiculous amount.

In Hull, some agents will provide the floorplans for free and some others will do them for £50.

3. Viewings

All viewings should be accompanied and by appointment only. If there happens to be an existing tenant in situ, they should be given at least 24 hours' notice prior to any viewing.

Will your lettings agent keep you updated on how the viewings have gone? If they do, then how often will you be updated?

You should not have to chase your lettings agent for feedback every time. It is important to set these parameters beforehand, otherwise it'll just lead to a lot of miscommunication.

Viewings are about the quality. If the agent is good at their job and the marketing, advertising and customer service is impeccable, then your property should let relatively quickly and not many viewings will take place.

A general rule of thumb is that if 10 viewings take place and there has not been an offer then something isn't quite right, either with the marketing or the pricing.

If so, then is the wording on the advert right? If the advert says 'quiet' yet the property is on a main road, then this will make applicants feel misled and unlikely to want the property.

Is the pricing right? If not, then get the agent to reduce the price immediately.

Obtaining feedback from viewings will help identify what the challenge is and the agent should be able to provide you with a cost-effective solution to any obstacle.

4. Offers

All offers received must be legally advised to the landlord. Do not be tempted to take the first offer if you or the lettings agent have any doubts about the suitability of the tenant or the offer made.

It is easy to just accept the first offer that comes, yet there are a couple of things that you will need to consider before accepting.

Will the tenant be moving in straight away?

The aim is to have minimal void periods. For example, if your property is being advertised for £500 a month. You receive an offer for £500, but the tenant cannot move in for four weeks. You also receive an offer for £480 and the tenant can move in straight away. This means you will get your rent quicker. Also note that it will take 24 months to recuperate the difference in that four-week void just so you can get a tenant paying £500 rather than £480.

Also, bear in mind that it is traditionally more challenging to find tenants during the summer holidays and the Christmas period.

Although the agent will reference the tenants properly, you will want to consider the following questions:

- Who are the tenants?
- What do they do for a living?
- How old are they?
- Will they respect your property?
- Will they be able to pay the rent each month?
- Do they need any furniture to be provided for the tenancy?

Your agent should have a good gut feeling about the tenants and you should trust their judgement.

5. Deposits

Deposits are often a source of debate and following a recent change in the law, all tenancy deposits must be placed into either the Governmental Custodial Scheme, or a Government Approved Scheme Provider.

The main three are:

- Deposit Protection Service (DPS)
- My Deposits
- Tenancy Deposit Scheme (TDS).

The law in England changed on 1st June 2019. The section below is direct from the Association of Residential Letting Agents website.

Tenant Fees Act

The Tenant Fees Act sets out the Government's approach to banning letting fees for tenants.

The key measures of the Act include:

- *Tenancy Deposits must not exceed the equivalent of five weeks' rent (unless the annual rent exceeds £50,000 – in which case, deposits are capped at six weeks' rent).*
- *Holding Deposits will be capped at no more than one week's rent.*
- *The amount that can be charged for a change to a tenancy will be capped at £50, unless the landlord demonstrates that greater costs were incurred.*
- *The Consumer Rights Act 2015 is amended to specify that the letting agent transparency requirements should apply to third-party websites.*

Alongside rent and deposits, agents and landlords will only be permitted to charge tenants fees associated with:

- *A change or early termination of a tenancy when requested by the tenant.*
- *Utilities, communication services and Council Tax.*
- *Payments arising from a default by the tenant where they have had to replace keys or a respective security device, or a charge for late rent payment (not exceeding 3% above the Bank of England base rate).*

A breach of the fees ban will be a civil offence with a financial penalty of up to £5,000.

You could always get your prospective tenant to get a guarantor. That way if there are any challenges with rental payments or late payment of rent, the guarantor will then become liable instead.

6. References

Referencing tenants is fundamental. Poor referencing can often lead to poor tenants. It doesn't matter where in the country you invest, poor tenants are not good for your property.

An agent should obtain as much information as possible on any prospective tenant. This information should include a reference from:

- A relative and/or previous landlord.

- An employer (preferably the tenant should be under some form of contracted employment and have been at the company for over three months).
- Their previous three months' bank statements. A general rule of thumb is if their take-home pay is over 150% of the monthly rent, then there should be no issues in the rent being paid.
- Some form of photographic identification.
- A simple credit check. (This will reveal whether the prospective tenant has any county court judgements (CCJs) against their name).

Circumstances change. A great tenant may suffer a family bereavement or lose their job. These situations happen in life and it is important to remember that effective communication can solve a lot of challenges. If circumstances do change, then your agent should have the skills to be able to show empathy and manage the situation so that you are still able to get your rent.

TOP TIP – Obtaining a homeowner guarantor as well will provide extra security for you knowing that you can legally chase the guarantor should the tenant consistently not pay the rent.

7. Tenancy Agreement

The agent should provide an Assured Shorthold Tenancy (AST) Agreement, that complies with all current legal requirements for tenancies.

If you have any extra stipulations or suggestions, then you should be able to work with your agent in order to implement them into the AST. For example, you might want to include the fact that the tenant is allowed certain pets, such as dogs and cats, in the property.

Please note that in Scotland you will have Private Residential Tenancies (PRT's) rather than AST's. AST's are in England and Wales.

8. Rent Collection

The agent will collect the rent on your behalf. The agent will also have systems in place for chasing up any delays in payments too.

What systems does your agent have in place? Do they ring the tenant? Do they text the tenant? Do they have an escalation stage? (i.e. text followed by e-mail followed by letter followed by a house visit.)

At the end of the day, you are running a property business and rental income is the lifeblood. Your agent will have good systems in place for chasing up rent, should be prompt in paying you your rent, and providing you with a written statement of account each month.

Work with your lettings agent to establish a payment date for your rent. Having an established date will save you from chasing up your agent frequently.

9. Inventory

An inventory may not be essential if your property is unfurnished, yet will be essential if your property is partly or fully furnished.

The agent should be able to provide an inventory service so that both they and the tenant are aware of what is in the property at the time of moving in and to record any defaults or defects that the property may have (for example, a mark on the carpet or a chipped worktop surface). All of these will be recorded.

The agent should also perform a pre-checkout inventory on your property. This will occur when the agent has received notice to vacate from the tenant and will involve advising the tenant of what they will need to do in order to get their full deposit returned.

This can save an awful lot of time and aggravation later as it is common for disputes to arise with the repayment of deposits.

10. Your new home

It is good practice for the agent to go around with the tenant on moving-in day in order to show them how the facilities in the property work, where the stopcock(s) are in case of emergency, and give them a list of contact numbers for the council/utility companies as well as the agent's emergency contact number.

An extensive tenancy pack should be included on the day that the tenants move in and all of this information should be in it.

11. Setting up bills

The agent should be able to arrange for payment of items such as service charge, water rates and insurance on the landlord's behalf, at the landlord's request.

In Hull, our lettings agents will help the tenants set up the council tax, electric and gas bills and the water bills. Having an agent that will do this is great for your time and your peace of mind.

12. Repairs and emergencies

You're on holiday and having the time of your life. The phone rings – there's a leaky tap. You're in Barbados. The tap needs sorting. Cue annoyed family members and friends as you spend the next three hours trying to find a local plumber to fix the tap!

This is where a good lettings agent really becomes worth their weight in gold.

Minor repairs (£100 or less in Hull, around £200 or less in London) should be dealt with by the agent through their list of local tradesmen. The repairs then normally come off the rental income statement.

For major works (over £200), the agent must obtain quotations for the work for your perusal and the agent should obtain at least three quotes for the works. Once completed, you should also receive all the necessary receipts as this will keep both your accountant and HMRC happy.

What is the agent's policy for dealing with emergencies? Do they have a 24-hour phone number? If an inappropriate call is made, will the tenant be charged? Or will you be charged?

The agent needs to be firm and fair with the tenants – not abusive or controlling, but very good at effectively managing the tenant.

When a tenant moves out, you should be prepared to pay to bring the property back up to scratch. Normally, this will include replacing items such as lightbulbs, small remedial works and having the property professionally cleaned.

It is always important to keep your property in superb condition. By doing this, you'll be able to achieve the maximum rent and the chances are that you will attract a better class of tenant.

It all comes down to psychology. If you are moving into a house that is very tidy and well-presented, then the chances are that you will be tidy and well presented too. If you are moving into a property that is untidy, scruffy and a bit rough around the edges, then the chances are that you will be the same too.

If you neglect your property, you enter into a downward spiral whereby you have difficulty getting tenants and keeping them. A happy tenant in a well-maintained property will most likely stay longer.

Top Tip 1 – Budget for a light refurb for every three to five years. Keeping on top of your property is important and keeping it looking fresh is very useful.

Top Tip 2 – A good practice would be to set aside 10% of the monthly rent. This can sit in a reserve account and covers MOE (Monthly Operating Expenses). This means that when a challenge arises or a light refurb needs doing, then you're not scrambling around trying to find the finance.

13. Inspections

Will your lettings agent inspect the property and report back to you?

They should: any good lettings agent should inspect the property at least once a quarter and send a report to you.

Having reports is superb for being able to know what is going on, what condition the property is in and helps you to maintain the quality of the property.

It also means small problems can be dealt with before they become large ones!

14. Notices

The agency should be able to assist you in the issuing of notices to vacate the property, and advise of receipt of any notice to vacate sent by the tenants. A Section 8 (where the landlord wants the property back from the tenant and wishes to do this via obtaining a possession order from the court, thereby ending the tenancy agreement) and Section 21 (a notice which a landlord must give to the tenant to begin the process to take back possession of a property let on an AST) are relatively straightforward to fill out, yet most people will ask their agent or a property solicitor to do them. This is because any incorrect procedures or information that are provided will mean that the serving of the notice is invalid.

Any good agent will know how to legally evict a tenant and what notices need to be served at what time. There are strict procedures that need to be followed.

I have been lucky enough never to have had to use a Section 8 or 21 notice and the eviction process can be quite costly. Please do not be under the illusion that it is an easy process. Most of time they can be straightforward, but there are times when it can be extremely costly as you will have to take into consideration court fees, tribunal fees and lack of incoming rent throughout the process.

https://www.gov.uk/evicting-tenants/section-21-and-section-8-notices

The Gov.uk website is really helpful as well.

At the time of writing, the Government is looking into the idea of abolishing Section 21 in England and Wales. From the people that I have spoken to, they believe that this idea could have catastrophic consequences.

There is no guarantee that Government will abolish the use of Section 21 notices.

It is advisable that you keep up to date with the NLA, RLA, ARLA, Property 118 and property news in general so that you know what is going on, what is being proposed and how to work with such changes in legislation, policies and procedures.

15. Legislation

The agency should keep up to date with any legal changes that might affect the landlord and advise how this might affect you. There are so many agents out there that really have no idea what is going on and this is not good and not fair on you.

It is important for you to have a basic understanding of what is going on, yet more important for your agent to know the ins and outs.

You would have spoken to various lettings agents during your initial area research and therefore you should have a very good understanding of which lettings agents will be in your area and which ones will do a good job. You will still have to work with the lettings agent and make sure that the lettings agent can still do a good job.

A lettings agent should always be a part of your power team and you should not take them for granted. Work closely with them, do your due diligence on them and nurture and manage the relationship. As with anything in life, it can be a case of trial and error.

A great lettings agent will make you a lot of money over time.

Professional Property Bodies and Licencing

Professional Property Bodies

Not every landlord or lettings agency belongs to a professional body. It is my personal belief that they should do for the purpose of best practice.

It is important to note that if you are buying investment properties in Wales, then it is a legal obligation to register yourself as a landlord as per Part 1 of the Housing (Wales) Act 2014.

Go to https://www.rentsmart.gov.wales/en/landlord/landlord-registration/ in order to find out how to register.

At the time of writing, it is not a legal requirement in England or Scotland (yet!).

If you are investing in England then you should seek to join the National Landlords' Association (NLA) or Residential Landlords' Association (RLA) as they have a plethora of online content, training and documents.

In their own words, the NLA is here to: *help our members navigate these challenges and proudly offer some of the most comprehensive learning resources and market-leading intelligence available in the sector. Our collective experience and the inclusive, wide-ranging reach of our organisation, combined with a wealth of online products and value-added services is why we call ourselves The Knowledge Network.*

We seek a fair legal and regulatory environment for both landlord and tenant, and actively lobby the government on behalf of our members. In addition, our representatives run regular branch meetings and landlord courses in over 100 locations throughout the UK and also provide an important link for our members with local authorities and fellow landlords.

If you are investing in Scotland, then you should also seek to join the NLA or the Scottish Association of Landlords (SAL) by going to their website which is https://scottishlandlords.com/advice/

Being a part of the NLA myself, it represents good value for money. The RLA is similar and most landlords will either sign up with one or the other, though not necessarily both.

You can also join your local landlords' association (if there is one). This is highly recommended too.

Selective Licencing

Selective licencing can occur in certain parts of the country. Selective licencing is required for ANY houses within a designated area where the whole of the house is occupied under a single tenancy or licence, or under two or more tenancies or licences in respect of different dwellings contained in it.

The cost and conditions of having such a licence will vary from local authority to local authority. Throughout your networking and research, it is important to find out whether or not your area has any selective licencing.

NB – Please do NOT get confused between selective licencing and HMO licencing because they are two completely different things with two different sets of criteria.

Summary

In a nutshell, a good lettings agent should ensure your property is hardly ever empty, take over most of the responsibility of looking after your property and come to you with solutions, not problems.

This level of service leaves you free to get on with the tasks of research, financing and negotiation of the purchase of your next property.

You must register yourself as a landlord in Wales and you must (in Scotland) check to see if your lettings agent is on the agency list. If you decide to self-manage in Scotland then you will need to register too.

Ensure that your property has the necessary certifications in place and also do your research to see if your property is in an area where selective licencing is applicable.

Congratulations: What To Do Next!

First of all, congratulations for buying your first property and getting yourself on the property investment ladder.

Please do let me know how you have done, by contacting me on:

Instagram – www.instagram.com/robert_smallbone_1988/

LinkedIn – www.linkedin.com/in/robert-smallbone-5a4186114/

Facebook – www.facebook.com/robsmallbone88

Like The Property Nomads' Podcast Facebook Page:
https://www.facebook.com/ThePropertyNomadsPodcast/

You can do many different things now that you have successfully purchased your first investment property.

You may decide that you do not want to buy any more properties and that your first investment property will be enough. Although I would strongly urge you to think differently and go out and buy more, I will fully respect that decision if this is the decision that best suits your needs and wants.

However, you are now knowledgeable in how to buy a property, renovate it and then rent it out. You should ideally repeat the process and buy another one, maybe more. Ideally, you will buy it in a very similar area to where you have just bought your first one. This way, you can use the same lettings agent and will be able to use your power team to its maximum potential.

You could decide to get a property mentor in order to guide you and push you even further. I've been getting mentored on and off since January 2017 and a good mentor is worth their weight in gold. A good mentor will be a few steps ahead of you and will be able to hold you accountable and will be able to push you even further.

If you would like to know more about The Property Nomads' Mentorship packages, then e-mail the team at rob@thepropertynomads.com.

You may decide that you want to further your knowledge and get some professional training in order to understand more about property and the different strategies and ways in which to invest in property.

It is not the purpose of this book to tell you where to go or what you have to do. I can only advise you based on my personal experiences and what I have found out and learned throughout all my trainings and education.

Congratulations once again. Now, go and repeat the process!

A Friendly Realistic Reminder

Property investing is one of those industries where things are likely to go wrong – for example, an estate agent or lettings agent not doing their job properly, a boiler breaking down, a tenant damaging a property or having a void period.

These things are part and parcel of this industry that you're getting yourself into.

Work on your mindset and realise that everything that happens in life can be treated objectively or subjectively. We can make whatever we want out of a situation. We are in control of our emotions and our reactions.

When you come across a void period, a difficult tenant or someone not doing their job properly, then just remember to always act cool and calm and come to a sensible conclusion.

Just remember, any event in our life is objective yet our reactions are subjective. Our reactions are whatever we want them to be. This will hold you in good stead moving forward in property.

Property Training

Property training is essential if you are looking to progress to the next level. This book has given you an in-depth process of how to buy your first buy-to-let. In order to build your buy-to-let portfolio, you can simply rinse and repeat this process.

If you are looking to do different strategies in property, then it would be wise to read books on those strategies and possibly attend courses based around those strategies.

Other Property Strategies

There are many different property strategies out there, including:

- HMO (House of Multiple Occupation).
- Rent-to-Rent.
- Lease Options.
- Land Development.
- Rent-to-Buy.
- Buy-to-Sell (Flipping).
- Commercial Conversions.
- Property Sourcing.
- Deal Packaging.
- Build-to-Rent.
- Serviced Accommodation.

There are many different specialists in each different niche. The above list is certainly not exhaustive.

Many property investors will cut their teeth on buy-to-lets before undertaking a new property strategy. Some people will do buy-to-lets and just stick with them, and some people will never do buy-to-lets and go straight for another investment method instead.

Mentorship

Mentorship. Why would you need a mentor? Why would you want a mentor?

When I first started in property I was a bit lost, a bit confused and had no great sense of direction. Despite buying property number one, it felt as though no progress had been made. Therefore, I decided to invest into a mentorship programme. It was a simple 30-day rolling contract and my mentor at the time really helped me to focus on myself, my visions and my values.

My visions and values were slightly re-aligned and this gave me a new impetus into the business and really helped to get me back into the game of property.

Having someone to guide you along the way, and being able to learn from their mistakes, is invaluable. It is often compared to standing on the shoulders of giants, and with good reason.

After a great 12 months we parted ways, because my mentor had brought me up to the level I wanted to be and had constructively pushed my boundaries and helped to alter my mindset.

When you come across the chance to be mentored by someone who is an expert in your field, then you should take that opportunity.

The 4C's That ANY Mentor Should Have

Mentorship is an incredibly powerful thing in anyone's life. If you have the drive and desire to want to succeed and take your business and life to the next level, then you will want to be mentored in order to achieve that.

Imagine being able to accelerate your growth and success by standing on the shoulders of giants and being able to leverage your time by learning from the mistakes of others.

Some of the common reasons why people decide to invest in property are: because they want financial freedom, time freedom and to be able to create a lifestyle from relatively passive income.

These are great reasons to invest in property as an asset class.

If you had the chance to achieve what you wanted to achieve, but to do it in a shorter space of time then would you want to do that? I'm pretty sure that you would.

You will have your own reasons as to why you want to invest in property or why you are already investing property, and you may be asking yourself why you would even need a mentor?

Why Would You Need A Mentor?

There are many reasons why you would need a mentor.

Some people will go on many training courses, will learn and then take action. Some people will not do any training and will just learn as they go along. They may end up making more mistakes, but they are happy with what they are doing and achieving.

Some people will not take action or will be scared of buying their first investment property and will have so many questions and queries.

Some people just want someone to hold their hand so that they can learn.

You may have such a strong desire to succeed, and such a strong reason 'why', that you just understand that the right mentor will help you to the very echelons that you have been dreaming of.

Maybe you struggle with accountability in your business and you know that a mentor will hold you accountable and help you to push yourself forward.

Maybe your partner in life doesn't understand property. Maybe your partner is just not interested in property as it is your "thing". It is possible that this means that you need someone else in your life: someone that understands property and has a genuine interest in property. A mentor would be a good person for this.

Property can be an incredibly lonely journey, so having someone to work with and learn from is invaluable.

How Do You Find a Mentor?

There are many ways in which you can find a property mentor. You may find a potential property mentor at Property Investor Networking (PIN) meetings, Progressive Property Networking (PPN) meetings, Business Networking International (BNI) meetings and any other business or property-related networking events.

A property mentor may be writing a blog or have written a book or two.

Social media is very powerful nowadays. You can always search on social media sites such as Facebook, LinkedIn, Twitter, Instagram, etc. for a property mentor.

In all fairness, you are more likely to find a property mentor on Facebook or LinkedIn due to the more professional nature of the sites.

You may find a property mentor by listening to property podcasts or by attending training courses.

As with many things in life though, word of mouth recommendations are the best way to find a property mentor. Speak to others that are involved in property investing, and ask if they have been mentored or if they can give you a personal recommendation.

When I started getting mentored, I found my mentor through Facebook.

The 4C's That ANY Mentor Should Have

Ok, so you know why you need a property mentor and you have now found a property mentor. What do you do next?

It is not just a case of finding someone, asking them to mentor you and then that is that. Far from it.

As with any friendship or relationship, it will take time. You want to work with someone that you like and can trust. You ideally (although not necessarily) want to have something else in common that isn't just property and success.

I have developed a 4C's model that you must follow in order to find the right mentor for you:

Credibility

Any mentor must have credibility – property credibility. Your mentor must be a step ahead of you in terms of property and must have some 'skin in the game'. For example, at the time of writing, I've accumulated over 20 properties in just over three years, 16 of which are buy-to-lets.

These numbers sound good, but you will want to know that the information is accurate. This is where word-of-mouth recommendations and social media research become very important.

Does your potential mentor have a Facebook Page or an online presence such as a website?

Just because someone says they have something, it doesn't mean that they actually do. Check them out, do your research. How credible are they? Do they have what they say they have? Are they who they say they are?

Congruency

Does the mentor say they are going to do something and then do it? Does the mentor act and talk in the same way? Are they talking about buy-to-let investing and actually investing in buy-to-let themselves?

Congruency is very important when it comes to picking a mentor to work with.

You may want to be mentored in buy-to-lets, HMO's, Land Development, Commercial Conversions, etc.

For example, if you have two buy-to-lets and want to have more in your portfolio, then you would want to consider me to mentor you as I am involved in 17 buy-to-lets. If you wanted to get more involved in commercial conversions, then you would not want to consider me to mentor you as it is not a strategy that I have done.

Your mentor should be talking the talk and walking the walk. This is where research is incredibly important as well. Don't always take people's word for it. Do your due diligence into your mentor in order to make sure that what they say they do, and what they are actually doing, are the same thing.

Commitment

You want (and deserve) a mentor that is as committed to your success as you are. What is the point in being committed to your success if your mentor is not?

There are too many stories out there where people have paid for a mentorship only for the mentor to then show no drive or desire to help. That is absolutely shocking and unfortunately it does happen.

Any good mentor will be committed to you, your success, your portfolio and to help you achieve what you want to achieve.

Knowing that you have someone to share ideas with, mastermind with and to learn from is incredibly important.

Having a bad mentor can leave a bad taste in your month and make you lose focus. This is not good.

How will you know if your mentor is committed?

Do your research. See them speak on stage, check out their online videos, check out their website and social media profiles and make sure that they will hold you accountable by task setting and having frequent Skype calls or one-to-one meetings. Speak to them on the phone as well. You will able to tell instinctively whether that mentor is the right person for you.

Contract

Contracts are incredibly important. You may have a mentor that works on a non-contract basis (eg. for a monthly fee). That is ok as long as you are happy with this and you do not pay more than a month in advance.

Most mentors will have a contract. If they don't (and they want to charge you a large amount and NOT work on a month-by-month basis), then you should walk away.

When you go into a shop and swap money for goods or a service, is it fair to say that you would want a receipt for those goods or services? EXACTLY!

Mentorship is no different. You will want to have a contract in place so that you know the terms and conditions and what to expect from your mentor. The contract will lay out what is expected of everyone involved and what you get for your money.

Every mentor will be different with what they offer. At the end of the day, as long as you are happy with your money being exchanged for that mentorship service and you are happy with the contract in place, then that is all that matters.

The Property Nomads Can Help YOU!

The Property Nomads offer mentorship packages and programmes. Find out more by contacting rob@thepropertynomads.com

BONUS 1 - THE TOP 8 PROPERTY BOOKS THAT YOU NEED TO READ

There are so many books out there. So much information to read. So many new things to learn.

This list is NOT a definitive list. It is simply the top eight property books I believe that you need to read (or listen to if you would prefer to do so on Audible).

If you spoke to 100 different people and asked them to name their top property books, then it is very likely that you would get 100 different combinations.

Every book in this list is very useful in its own right. The books in this list cover a wide range of advice and knowledge from various property experts.

If you have already read these books, then find the time to read them again.

These books will provide you with knowledge and action points that will help you to change your life.

At the time of writing, The Property Monks do not have a book but this will change in the future. Look out for e-mails about new book releases.

1. *Rich Dad Poor Dad* by Robert Kiyosaki

One of the most – if not *the* most – influential books in the world. The fundamental knowledge provided in this book is life-changing. The different ways in which to think of assets and liabilities and how to get assets working for you is mind-blowing.

2. *The Complete Guide to Property Investing* by Rob Dix

Rob Dix provides really good, quality content in this book. *The Complete Guide to Property Investing* provides exceptional knowledge whilst combining good action points and things to get you started in property.

3. *How To Make Cash in a Property Crash* by Rob Moore and Mark Homer

Speaking from experience, Rob and Mark provide you with useful property strategies and ways to make money whilst everyone else is being fearful. Booms and busts are both part of the economic cycle. Know what you are doing, play your cards right and you will be able to profit nicely when the economy is in a downturn.

4. *Property Magic* by Simon Zutshi

The best part of this book is the ethical stance which Simon takes. In all fairness, we should all be ethical in property and look to create win-win situations where possible. This book outlines Simon's journey and provides some great example deals that he (and others) have had. *Property Magic* also outlines the various property strategies that exist.

5. *100 Property Investing Secrets* by Rob Dix

A simple, yet very effective, book. Rob Dix provides the bulk of the content and guest writers have complemented this by offering their advice too. The book covers a wide variety of subjects and gives insights into the challenges of property and how to overcome them. An easy read, packed with many useful hints and tips.

6. *44 Closely Guarded Property Secrets* by Rob Moore and Mark Homer

This book is a compilation of Rob, Mark and many guest writers. They all come together to bring a plethora of knowledge, ideas and challenges that they have had in property. They bring the solutions too! This book covers a wide range of topics and has some very useful action points.

7. *Planning and HMOs* by C.J Haliburton

If you are considering a change of property use and are looking to buy, renovate or manage HMOs (Houses of Multiple Occupation) then read this book. Jim Haliburton has a no-nonsense approach to writing and gets straight to the point in this book. It's packed full of useful and relevant information.

8. *Multiple Streams of Property Income* by Rob Moore and Mark Homer

If you are looking to gain multiple streams of property income such as speaking, running a training academy etc., then you will definitely want to read this. The fundamentals in this book are really useful and provide a superb insight into how you can use your existing knowledge to earn more money in a variety of ways.

Personally, I love to read and gain knowledge. These books all have their strong points and will provide you with some fantastic insider information and action points. No matter where you are in your property journey or whether you are just curious, take action and read these books.

BONUS 2 - THE TOP 5 PROPERTY AND BUSINESS PODCASTS YOU NEED TO LISTEN TO

What is a podcast?

A podcast is a digital audio file made available on the Internet for downloading.

Did you know that only 4% of people in the UK listen to podcasts?

Why do you need to listen to them?

Podcasts provide great quality content for you to listen to. Imagine being able to listen to material while driving or at the gym or even commuting. Podcasts can help you to further your knowledge in a particular subject and provide key action points too.

Podcasts are essentially a different way of learning and an alternative to physically reading. If you listen to them on the go, then you will be leveraging your time.

How can you listen to them?

You can access podcasts through the iTunes store or the Android store. Podcasts are completely free.

You can listen to them on any audio device such as a phone, computer or a tablet. You can listen to them on numerous speeds. 2x speed may take some time to get used to, but that is what you need to aim for. That way you will be able to listen to double the content in the same amount of time.

The Top 5 Property/Business/Life Podcasts You Need To Listen To

1. The Property Nomads Podcast by Rob Smallbone and Matt McSherry

The Property Nomads Podcast provides a blend of property, travel and business-related information, tips and tricks and interviews with a variety of business and property people. You can subscribe to The Property Nomads Podcast for FREE on:

iTunes – https://apple.co/2UdfXXY

Stitcher – https://bit.ly/2uC2RVr

Spotify – https://spoti.fi/2Wvxk3I

The Property Nomads Podcast is on most podcast platforms so come and check us out, subscribe and share with your friends and family.

2. The Disruptive Entrepreneur by Rob Moore

Rob Moore has built up multiple businesses and multiple streams of property income. The Disruptive Entrepreneur is designed to share a plethora of knowledge with you and covers many topics from brand building all the way through to how to deal with angry customers.

The content is a mixture of interviews, short podcasts and some live Q & A sessions. The podcast isn't focused on property, but instead focuses on general business and entrepreneurship. It is well worth listening to and there are always golden nuggets of information.

3. The Tim Ferriss Show by Tim Ferriss

The Tim Ferriss Show is absolutely fantastic and covers a wide variety of content. Tim is a venture capitalist and has a plethora of knowledge in a multitude of areas. The podcasts have covered topics such as sexual equality, the use of drugs, physics and has very good interviews with key people such as Jack Dorsey (founder of Twitter) and so forth.

This is highly recommended for the hints, tips and tricks that you can get from listening to this content and for the sheer variety too.

4. Mark My Words by Mark Homer

Similar to the disruptive entrepreneur, Mark shares many live Q&A sessions and interviews in Mark My Words. The podcast is predominantly property-focused and is intricate in detail (just like Mark himself). You will always learn something new by listening to this podcast either from Mark or one of the special guests.

Topics covered include: property tax planning, changes in government legislation and how to live a low-cost high life.

5. The Inside Property Investing Podcast by Mike Stenhouse

Mike mainly interviews others and gets them to share their journeys on this podcast. This property podcast has special guest interviews, site interviews and studio interviews that cover a wide range of property journeys and strategies. It is great to hear and share the successes of others and this podcast will be able to inspire to you take your property business and knowledge to the next level.

BONUS 3 - EIGHT LIFE HACKS TO HELP YOU FOCUS MORE

As humans it is very easy to become overwhelmed because we decide to take on too much in too short a space of time. Some people enjoy it, some don't. Here are eight life hacks to help you focus more:

1. KNOW your visions and values + KNOW what you want

Knowing why you are doing something is important. Knowing what your values are is also very important. If you know that your values are property investing, family and physical health, then this will make your decisions easier moving forwards.

For example, if you get invited out with a group of friends and have a choice of going out or doing your Rightmove research so that you can start your investment journey. If your highest value is property investing, then you will do your research rather than go out.

2. Get rid of distractions

Put your phone on airplane mode! This is easier said than done because we live in age of technology and distractions.

(Take me back to the 13 or 14th Century when there were no social media distractions – just the plague instead!)

While writing this book, I turned off my phone for five days. It was incredibly liberating and I got a ridiculous amount of work done as well.

3. Stick to your diary/time management – stick to the routine and don't change it for anyone

Routine = results. If you work full-time, then chances are that you will already have some form of routine. It is imperative that you are able to fit property investing into your routine. Make time for it no matter what!

4. Trust other people to do things – this will give you more focus on the job in hand and other people can grow other areas of your business for you.

This is effectively utilising leverage to its maximum potential. If you are able to put trust in others, then this will put you in great stead for moving forward in life and in property. You have to be able to make time by leveraging the skills and expertise of others.

Maybe you WILL get that lettings agent to manage your property, maybe you will pay a cleaner to clean your house so that you can focus on other tasks such as putting in offers on property and researching property/overseeing your portfolio. We all have the same amount of time in a day, yet how we use that is very different.

Trust others and leverage their expertise.

5. Reward yourself when a goal is achieved – as entrepreneurs, we sometimes don't reward ourselves.

Having light at the end of the tunnel is crucial in order to keep yourself going mentally. During the goal-setting process, you should be setting rewards for yourself. Your rewards will have to be something that will get you going. Maybe you do not enjoy viewing property, but you know that if you view 20 properties in a week then you will treat yourself and your spouse to a nice meal in that new restaurant?

Maybe you will go on a family holiday when you have purchased and tenanted your 10th buy-to-let property? Your goals and rewards will be whatever make you tick. Just make sure that you set them!

6. Do not fear missing out (also known as FOMO)

This works hand in hand with number 2. Many people are addicted to their phones and easily get distracted because of a fear of missing out. You must have this mental battle and realise that you will sometimes miss out in life, you may reply to an email too late and miss out on a property deal. That happens. It's life. Win that battle with your mind and accept the fact that you will miss out on something every once in a while.

7. Know how much your time is worth and delegate tasks

There is a formula for working out how much your time is worth. Divide your salary (if you are working part of full-time) by the amount of hours that you work and you will have your hourly rate.

In order to delegate tasks effectively, you will want to delegate tasks that cost less than your hourly rate. i.e. If your hourly rate is £15 and it costs a cleaner £10 per hour to clean your house, then it is better to pay the cleaner. This is because if you do it, it will cost you £15 but if a cleaner does it then you will have saved £5. You will, more importantly, have gained time in order to focus on more money-making tasks such as portfolio management, booking viewings or working with your property power team.

8. Work in chunk time (i.e. work in one-hour slots)

Working in chunk time is proven to increase your efficiency and effectiveness. Compartmentalise your time as best you can. For example, when writing this book it took me about five days of intense work and I was writing in 23-minute slots followed by five minutes' rest. I repeated this about 15 times a day for five days and it certainly worked.

GLOSSARY

AST – Assured Shortland Tenancy

BMV – Below Market Value

D2V – Direct To Vendor

DUV – Done Up Value

EPC – Energy Performance Certificate

FOMO – Fear Of Missing Out

FTB – First-Time Buyer

GDV – Gross Development Value

HCC – Hull City Council

HLA – Humber Landlords' Association

HMO – House of Multiple Occupation

IO – Interest Only

JV – Joint Venture

LO – Lease Option

LTV – Loan To Value

MIMO – Money In, Money Out

NET ROI (Net Return On Investment)

NLA – National Landlords' Association

NMLI – No Money Left In

OPM – Other People's Money

PA – Per Annum

PCM – Per Calendar Month

R2R – Rent To Rent

RLA – Residential Landlords' Association

ROCE – Return On Capital Employed

ROI – Return On Investment

SA – Serviced Accommodation

SAL - Scottish Association of Landlords

SDLT – Stamp Duty Land Tax

THE AUTHOR

Rob Smallbone is a successful property investor, traveller, author, speaker, property project manager and is co-host of The Property Nomads' Podcast.

Rob is also on the committee for the Humber Landlords' Association and has a passion for sharing his knowledge with others.

Rob has travelled to over 45 countries in his lifetime and his aim is to visit every country in the world before he is 50.

Rob's personal values of authenticity, integrity and congruency have served him well over the years and will continue to do so in the years ahead.

You can connect with Rob on various social media platforms:

Instagram – www.instagram.com/robert_smallbone_1988/

LinkedIn – www.linkedin.com/in/robert-smallbone-5a4186114/

Facebook – www.facebook.com/robsmallbone88

Check out and like The Property Nomads Podcast Facebook Page (https://www.facebook.com/ThePropertyNomadsPodcast/) as well, as we often run special competitions and give-away prizes! Do not miss out on these fantastic opportunities.

OUR SERVICES

The Property Nomads are here to help you. We are passionate about helping others to get started in property and we are delighted to be able to offer the following to you:

- TPN Round Table Monthly Property Mastermind.
- TPN Round Table Monthly Sourcing Mastermind.
- TPN Monthly Mentoring Programme.
- TPN 2-Day Intensive On-Patch Mentorship. (We go through your business, your plans and work with you to kickstart your journey).
- Project management in Hull. If you have purchased property in Hull and do not want to oversee the refurbishment, then we can help.
- Property Sourcing Start-Up Pack.
- Opportunities to Joint Venture with us;

Contact rob@thepropertynomads.com for more details.

You can also get your free Buy-to-Let Deal Analyser off our website by signing up to receive our newsletter. Visit www.thepropertynomads.com and get your free analyser today!

Check out and like The Property Nomads Podcast Facebook Page (https://www.facebook.com/ThePropertyNomadsPodcast/) as well as we often run special competitions and give away prizes! Do not miss out on these fantastic opportunities.

44956606R00108

Printed in Poland
by Amazon Fulfillment
Poland Sp. z o.o., Wrocław